IMPRINT CLASSICS

Walkabout

Arthur Upfield

ETT IMPRINT
Exile Bay

Published as an Imprint Classic by ETT Imprint 2026

First published by ETT Imprint, Exile Bay in 2021 in hardback
First paperback by ETT Imprint, Exile Bay in 2022
First ebook publication by ETT Imprint 2022

Copyright © William Upfield 2021

Compiled by Tom Thompson

This book is copyright. Apart from any fair dealing for the purposes of private study, research, criticism or review, as permitted under the Copyright Act, no part may be reproduced by any process without written permission. Enquiries should be addressed to the publisher, or through the official Upfield website on www.arthurupfield.com

ETT IMPRINT
PO Box R1906
Royal Exchange NSW 1225 Australia

ISBN 978-1-923527-15-7 (paper)
ISBN 978-1-922473-88-2 (ebook)

Text design by Hanna Gotlieb
Cover design Tom Thompson

for William & Francesca Upfield

The author, working as a boundary-rider on the South Australian-New South Wales dog-proof fence.

CONTENTS

Arthur Upfield: An Epitaph by Pamela Ruskin *7*
1 Patrolling the World's Longest Fence *14*
2 A Visit to Lake Frome *24*
3 Men, Sheep and Far Horizons *29*
4 Hosts hidden in the Bush *39*
5 Coming Down With Cattle *47*
6 An Australian Camel Station *55*
7 Trapping for Fur *60*
8 Angling for Swordfish *73*
9 This Jealous Land *83*
10 Walking the Cattle *93*
11 Pearling Town of the North-West *105*
12 The Vermin Fences of Western Australia *115*
13 Australian Geographical Society *125*
Acknowledgements *132*

The last known photographs of Arthur Upfield, taken in his Bowral home in October 1963, while working on *The Lake Frome Monster*.

ARTHUR UPFIELD: AN EPITAPH

Pamela Ruskin

To be a success in Australia, you must work somewhere else; for Australians are constitutionally unable to appreciate their own creative workers unless they are living abroad or dead. At present, I'm not interested in the former condition and I'm not really in a hurry to achieve the latter one.

Australia's ace mystery writer, Arthur Upfield, wrote that in a letter to me, six years ago. Now he has fulfilled the latter condition too, lying alone at his home in Bowral of a heart disease that had wrecked his health for the last four or five years. It remains to be seen whether death will bring him the sort of recognition he always hoped would come to him in Australia.

During his last years, Upfield did, in fact, acquire a great measure of the fame he had battled for so hard and so long. Consistently good reviews welcomed most of his new books, but, in contrast to the superlatives that were lavished on his work in America and Western Germany, and even in Great Britain, the more restrained praise offered by Australian reviewers, interlaced with a due appraisal of his limitations, seemed to him rather half-hearted. He resented very much the attitude that because he wrote mystery stories, he wasn't to be considered a serious writer.

Yet, above all, Upfield was an honest man; a craftsman who knew his own faults as a writer, admitted them freely and strove hard to correct them. He was human enough to dislike attention being drawn to them in print.

Arthur Upfield's success rested on one main plank. He created a detective whom Anthony Boucher, crime editor of the *New York Times Literary Magazine,* called "the most original fictional detective of the last 20 years". He was the suave, urbane half-aboriginal Detective Inspector Napoleon

Bonaparte who combined in himself the sensitivity and almost mystic intuition of his aboriginal mother, with the sophistication and educated intelligence of his white father.

It was Upfield's constant delight that his readers all over the world reacted to "Bony" much as a wider reading public had reacted to Sherlock Holmes, and thought of him as a real person. He received hundreds of letters addressed to "Bony", and even newspapermen, much to his amusement, would question him closely to find out more about this blue-eyed, courteous sleuth who bucked authority, never lost a case, and treated women as though they were all princesses.

Bonaparte was as Upfield told me very often a real person. He was based on the half-caste son of a station owner, on whose property in the Darling Downs the young Arthur worked. This man was, like Bony, university-trained and wholly civilised; yet he too felt the call of his mother's tribe, and possessed many of its skills. Bony is thus four-fifths fact and only one-fifth fiction.

Whatever the balance, Bony was the kingpin in the structure of Arthur's success. He knew it and was never tempted to write a book in any other form, although he did write four romantic novels in his early days, before Bony was conceived.

What sort of a man was Arthur Upfield?

He was a tough, irascible, wiry, man. He had slate-coloured eyes, a thin trap of a mouth and ears like jug handles. He spoke almost through clenched teeth and was thus the despair of radio interviewers. His truculence hid a good deal of shyness. He knew Australia as few know it today. His Australia was not the Australia of big cities, which he believed were pretty much the same everywhere and which he loathed anyway. He loved the outback; the hot thirsty plains baking under the sun, the endless quiet of the bush at night, the roistering companionship of the small country pub, where weeks of hard-earned wages went down the hatch in one glorious bender, ending in oblivion and a headache.

To meet, he was as dinkum an Aussie as you'd find anywhere; yet he was an Englishman. According to his own account, he was the black sheep of a yeoman Sussex family. He felt smothered by the prospect of the respectable white-collar life that awaited him there, and utterly refused to settle down. Armed only with an overweening passion for Dickens and H. G. Wells, implanted in him by a solicitor uncle, and a fierce independence, Upfield was shipped off to Australia with his family's relieved blessing and some letters of introduction which he disdained to use. Immediately he fell hopelessly in love with the outback. "I clung to it till my teeth fell out," he said later.

As the years passed, Upfield's knowledge of Australia grew. He worked a mule team and was a boundary rider on a camel station in Western Australia. He dug opals at Coober Pedy, carried his swag on a bicycle without pedals all over Queensland and New South Wales, picked grapes, sheared sheep and took a job as a shearers' cook while, encouraged by the owner's wife, he wrote his first book, *The House of Cain*.

In those days, every swaggie and station hand knew and loved the poems of Banjo Paterson, Henry Lawson and Adam Lindsay Gordon, and would recite and talk about their favourites round the campfire at night. This, Upfield was to say very often, was the true voice of Australia, and it showed a pride in the writers who belonged to Australia which is less evident to day.

After serving in the A.I.F. for more than four years of World War 1. Arthur was more than ever in love with his adopted country. It was about this time that he started writing, but his first novel wasn't published until 1928. Just before Christmas, 1963, his thirty-second novel was on the bookstalls. In those 35 years, Upfield worked and travelled, and battered his way to success. He wrote about Australia for *Wide World Magazine*. He was a contributor to *Walkabout* from the first issue, which came out in November 1934, at a time when Ernestine Hill, Bill Harney, Donald Thompson and Ion Idriess were also writing for it. Even before this, he had become a "special" writer for the Melbourne *Herald* and even wrote a racing serial for it, aided by the paper's racing staff.

If in his youth he was hard drinking, hard swearing and truculent, in his advanced years he mellowed considerably. Underneath his prickly exterior, he was a shy, affectionate and kindly man, who never forgot a kindness and never knew how to hold a grudge. He said of himself, "I'm like a summer fire. I flare up quickly but I never persist with hard feeling."

He had a wry, dead-pan sense of humour. Typical of this was a comment in one of the last letters I had from him: "I never use bad language. I only use Australian words!" He could always laugh at himself, uneasily signing autographs in a city store or submitting to radio and T.V. questions with forthright but agonised candour.

He was always rather cagey about his age. In a letter written in the late '50's he refers to an article in which I had said he was in his late sixties. "Hardly the late sixties," he wrote, "not yet!" But as *Who's Who* and other reference works give his birth date as 1888, he was every bit of that. He was sixty when he led a five thousand-mile expedition through the Kimberleys, in 1948, for the Australian Geographic Society (*Walkabout*, October, 1948).

Although his books were being published, early success eluded his grasp, and the bitterness of those first years of failure stayed with him always. When success did come, it came from abroad. America had just entered the Second World War, and thousands of G.I.'s were packed off to Australia. There was a tremendous surge of interest in the country "down-under", about which few Americans knew anything at all.

Upfield's agent offered his work to Doubleday and Company, and they snapped up six titles overnight. Mothers, sisters, aunts and cousins of G.I.'s eagerly welcomed Upfield and Bony, and he achieved best seller status within a very short time. Americans at home saw Australia through Upfield's eyes, and felt they knew the sort of towns where their boys were stationed.

It has been said that Arthur Upfield's descriptive writing is so vivid and alive that it gives a truer picture of Australia and Australians than does that of many of our more literary writers. Although he was a crime writer, his plots were generally weak, but his descriptions of the outback and the odd characters with whom he peopled it were superb. Maybe it was the Australia of yesterday, without the great sprawling cities and the vast population growth caused by post-war migration, but it was the Australia he knew.

It is no coincidence that critics all over the world acclaimed his backgrounds, with their sprinkling of bush lore, aboriginal customs and marvellous revelation of what he liked to call "the book of the bush". For example, his story of a lake, Lake Victoria in fact, which he told *in Death of a Lake,* and of animals and birds desperately trying to get to the last of the water, while dead bodies pile up in their thousands, is masterly. As almost every critic remarked, "the lake is the real hero of this novel." Upfield really saw this lake dry up, when he was working for a Mr. James Hole on a property above Wilcannia, and he never forgot the horror of it. When the book was published, Mr. Hole, to whom it was dedicated, was able to state unequivocally that nothing Upfield wrote about it was exaggerated.

His story of Broome and the death throes of the pearling industry was another outstanding success both here and in the States. It was *The Widows of Broome,* and the first of his books to appear under the Heinemann colophon, after his break with Angus and Robertson. It told readers of a colourful corner of Australia, quite different and virtually unknown to them. This of course was the essential ingredient of Upfield's popularity. Almost every "Bony" adventure took readers to a new part of Australia, where Upfield had lived and worked during some part of his rolling stone existence.

By 1953, the elusive fruits of successful authorship were coming to him, and he was able to say that he was one of a meagre four or five Australian authors living wholly from the proceeds of his books. For this he gave credit to the United States, and he was and still is, as far as I know, the only foreigner to be admitted as a full member of the Mystery Writers' Guild of America. Late in 1962, he showed me proudly a set of cuff links bearing the M.W.G. insignia, which had just been sent to him as a tribute to his contribution as a mystery writer. He was truly touched by this and he told me again of his ambition to be able to accept their invitation to the annual banquet of the Guild. He was never able to do so.

In the 1950's, the rest of the world interested in Australia became interested in Upfield. Western Germany published almost every title of his, first in hard covers and then in paperbacks and in serial form. Italy, Denmark, Finland, Holland, Argentina, Mexico and even Japan sought translation rights and published many titles. He was almost embarrassed when he received letters from learned German professors who wished to discuss with him details of aboriginal lore and to learn from him more of its *mystique*. Anyway his health was not, at this time, good enough to embark on so serious a correspondence.

About 10 years ago, several of his books were turned into a series of radio plays under the title, *Man of Two Tribes*. Two well-known Australians were concerned in this. One was actor Frank. Thring, somewhat miscast as "Bony" and Morris West, then head of the radio production firm that produced the series, who was to become an even more successful author than Upfield.

Upfield used the Kimberleys as the background for another successful novel, *Cake in the Hatbox*. In the last few years he lived in Airey's Inlet, then Bermagui and finally Bowral. All these locations he incorporated into books. His new-found prosperity didn't affect his way of life greatly, for his tastes remained simple. But one extravagance did give him considerable pleasure. Around 1952, when he was living at Airey's Inlet, he bought himself a second-hand but shiningly beautiful Daimler, which he kept in immaculate condition. He didn't drive it a great deal, but when he had to make a trip to Melbourne, he would dress himself up in his best suit and an old-fashioned grey homburg, and set off, sitting behind the wheel as proudly as any teenager with his first "bomb". He would park it at a garage on the outskirts of the city and continue the rest of the way in a taxi. He wouldn't risk his precious car in the "traffic inferno". After his first serious heart attack, he sold the Daimler rather sadly.

The swagman who pushed a bike across the dusty tracks of the outback became a much-sought-after author or storyteller, as he preferred it. But he was a rebel to the last. Like "Bony", he hated authority and never bowed to a boss. He thought writers should belong to a union to prevent their being exploited. Like "Bony", he put women on a pedestal and treated them with old-fashioned courtesy. When he met one that didn't belong on that pedestal, he merely said she was an exception. He was a religious man, but a nonconformist in his beliefs.

When time has blurred today's picture of Australian writing, will Upfield survive? His style was often bad and his plots were slow. He despised the literary graces and what he termed the "pretentiousness of the literary snobs". He wrote for the "ordinary people of Australia", and the ordinary people will still read his books for many years. In Upfield's work they will find the empty, undeveloped land which bred the tough, hard-living outback men and women he admired so much and wrote about so well.

Now Detective Inspector Napoleon Bonaparte has solved his last case and laid away his kurdaitcha boots forever. He has, I think, joined the immortals of detective fiction. Arthur Upfield would have asked no more of posterity.

Arthur Upfield, c. 1930

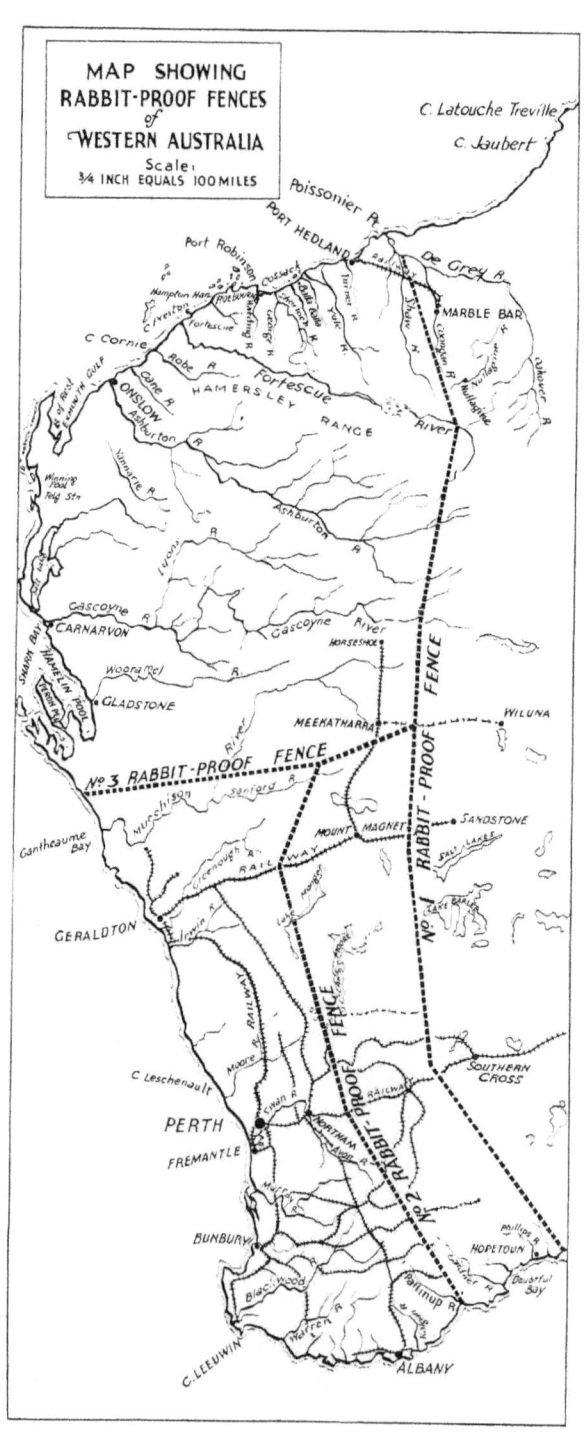

1.

PATROLLING THE WORLD'S LONGEST FENCE

Western Australia's 1100 Mile Rabbit-Proof Fence

IF it please you, accompany Millie and Curly and me on a patrol of one section of 163 miles of the longest fence in the world, the Number One Rabbit Fence, Western Australia. The purpose of such a fence, of which there are many in Australia, is to stop the migration of rabbits to the wheat belts. This particular fence begins at the edge of a water-washed rocky jetty facing the Southern Ocean, near Hopetoun, and it runs northward for 1,130 miles to end at a salt-water creek near Banningarra, on the North-west coast.

Millie and Curly are camels, almost akin to the elephant in intelligence, swayed by the human emotions of joy and anger controlled by a "homing" instinct almost as strong as that of the pigeon, at times placid and at other times as petulant as children. They are harnessed in tandem to a large, covered dray, which, when not drawn by them, is kept level with drop-sticks to provide the boundary rider with a one-room house on wheels.

At the northern extremity of the section, from which end the monthly patrol is made, is the Government Camel Station named Dromedary Hill, so called from the twin-backed, stony hill in the vicinity of the homestead. The man in charge comes with us the short distance to the fence through which we must pass to reach the narrow track flanking the fence on its east side for many hundreds of miles. Millie, the team leader, is turned to the south, and, when clear of the gate, the dray is stopped while *au revoirs* are exchanged by men who may not see another human soul for ten days or a fortnight.

Here we are able to view the fence and the track that form what is known as a cut line—a line first surveyed and then cleared to a width of twenty feet, the fence being then erected two feet west of the centre.

Northward the cut line dwindles to infinity in the dark mulga scrub. Excepting for a few angles to escape "break-aways" the cut line is rule straight.

Southward, the line narrows to a ribbon at the summit of a long rise nearly two miles distant, and beyond that rise, 161 miles away, is the small wheat town of Burracoppin on the main railway line from Perth to Kalgoorlie, which marks the southern extremity of this section. The fence runs a further 218 miles beyond the railway line to the Southern Ocean, whilst in the opposite direction it shears through the bush to the Indian Ocean, 750 miles distant.

We have to cover 326 miles before once again we see Dromedary Hill. Twenty-eight days the journey will occupy, and we will travel with the time-table regularity of trains. Down in Burracoppin, or wherever he may be, the inspector will know every evening where his riders are, or ought to be, camped.

Millie swings along, her tread cat-like and silent, placidly chewing her cud and quite resigned to the month's exile from all her friends and relatives at the station, but Curly, between the shafts of the dray, is not so resigned. He is, in fact, openly rebellious. He vents throaty growls, and endeavours to turn himself into the letter S in order to look back at those of his comrades that have come to the fence to watch us away, for be it understood that he wears winkers like any old dray horse.

Soon the homestead and the barren hills behind it are shut out by the bordering scrub. On the long slope, the wheels hiss softly in the deep, dry sand. The everlasting fence-posts slip by in endless procession.

We pass our first wooden mile-peg marked M/162 with the broad arrow beneath the numerals. Looking back and down the straight track, we can see a tiny dot midway between us and the vanishing point of the cut line. That dot is the Camel Station overseer, watching us until we disappear from his sight over the rise but a short distance ahead.

On the summit of the rise, the sand on the track is replaced with surface ironstone rock. Here the scrub trees thin out and give growth to the soft, pearl-grey flannel-bush, the salt-bush and the blue-bush, and the world-famed Western Australian everlasting flowers.

Round then the first angle of the fence at the 161-mile peg, to continue a further mile when the fence in turn forces us a trifle eastward.

There is no obvious reason why these angles should be made, but in all cases the real reason is that they are made to escape the precipitously faced break-aways. The dray wheels rumble hollowly over the surface rock, giving Curly a grand excuse to pretend to be frightened. As he is easily able to pull the dray himself without exertion, the brake is applied and he is given work to do.

To our right, through a veil of tree-branches, looms the sheer face of a Western Australian break-away caused in some far geological age by the subsidence of wide sections of the earth's crust. From here the track falls sharply at first, and then more gently in a perfectly straight line across comparatively open country to stab the heart of the bush spreading to the level, knife-edged horizon. The break-away cliff of red ironstone rock sweeps in a giant arc westward and then southward, appearing like the face of a great quarry, its summit fringed with scrub trees, its foot put down on white sand dotted with salt-bush. On the track, and out from the bordering bush, particles of mica reflect the sunlight from a billion points coloured white and gold and amber.

Down the stony slope, with hand on brake and eyes on the fence to detect a broken wire or a rent made in the netting by kangaroo or emu, we are hurried by the impetuous Curly, who would so like to break into a tearing gallop for a full mile— and then lie down for two or three days to get over it. When level ground is reached, the brake may be left alone, but never beyond jumping distance. It is astonishing how quickly a camel can spring into a gallop from a slow walk.

At length we reach the dense scrub, where no longer do the light of day and the reflection of the sun by the mica particles make buoyant our spirits. On both sides of the cut line, shadows fall between the trunks of living trees to the trunks and debris of dead timber. Save for a few crows that will follow us from camp to camp for many miles, and the ever-watching wedge-tailed eagles, mere specks against the sky, the world seems empty; it seems so, but is not really so.

Having of necessity left the Camel Station late this morning, we select our camp near the 156-mile peg, where the scrub provides a variety of food for the camels. A camel will not long eat of one kind of bush or tree leaf, and it will never eat grass, which is as well, because we shall see no grass until the farms are reached. It demands variety, and, if variety is not to be obtained, it will go hungry. Its habit is to wander from bush to tree, snatching a mouthful here and there and ignoring fodder on either side.

The dray is drawn just off the track. The wheels are chocked and the drop-sticks let down to ensure its level position after Curly is taken from between the shafts. Having been unharnessed, the camels are short-hobbled and permitted to roam.

This section of fence is the hardest of any for animals expected to live on the country. Its northern end at the Camel Station reaches the southern extremity of the pastoral country proper, and between that place and the salmon-gum country, first entered at the 60-mile post, extends a hundred-mile-wide belt of desert scrub, of low, tough bogeta and broombush, whereon no camel or horse or donkey will long maintain condition.

As there are no cross fences from one end of the section to the other, and as the camels will ever make back to the land of their birth, once they get away from the rider, he will be lucky to overtake them before they reach the Camel Station gate.

As they cannot be trusted to camp for the night at even one of the few good camel camps, it is necessary along this section to cut bush and drag it to selected trees, to which they are secured with long neck ropes that permit them to lie down. At one time a rider lost his camels at the 69-mile peg and was obliged to walk back to the 163-mile peg to get them again. One eats from a drop table in the dray to escape the ants. Save only when it rains, one sleeps on a Coolgardie stretcher set up beside the dray. At dawn, when the camels simultaneously get up, the clatter of their bells announces the new day. Before we dress, the mound of grey fire ash is broken open to reveal the red wood coals, on which is placed the billycan containing the remains of last night's tea; and, when the camels have been freed to find their breakfast, ink-black tea is sipped and a cigarette smoked. The sky is ever of interest as a weather prophet, excepting during the winter months when rain-bearing clouds often sweep across the clear sky without a heralding sign.

After a simple breakfast of bacon and damper and milkless tea, we pack all gear into the dray, and then, perhaps, a couple of posts are cut to replace posts which have become rotten. Every year hundreds of new posts are put in.

To-day we cross a spinifex plain—semi-globes of spiny bush covering the brown earth like large, green meat-covers.

Beyond the plain, we again enter the mulga timber, with the track and the fence dwindling to infinity ahead until we are able to see the blank wall of scrub at the angle marked by the 148-mile peg. Time drags before we reach the turn, and, having swung round it, we again see the fence dwindling to infinity amid the silver leaves of the broad-leafed mulga.

There is work to be done south of the 144-mile peg, where there is a rain-shed—a simple roof of corrugated iron from which rainwater is piped into two large receiving tanks beneath it. There are several of these rain-sheds on this section constructed for the fence-rider and his camels, and sometimes thoughtless and unauthorized travellers leave a tap running with the consequent waste of hundreds of gallons of precious water on which life itself depends.

Curly makes known his desire for a drink when within a quarter of a mile of the rain-shed. He strains against braked wheels, his haste objected to by Millie, who vents low rumbles of protest. Two hundred yards from the water, the dray is drawn off to the side of the track, because round about the rain-shed there is no wood for cooking and there is a super-abundance of ants.

At five-thirty the two drinking buckets are taken from the dray with purposeful noise. At once the bells strapped to the necks of the camels feeding deep in the bush cease their pleasing tinkle.

The buckets, continuing to be loudly rattled, are taken to the water tanks, when from a distance again comes the rhythmic tinkle quickly becoming louder until the two grey shapes appear at the edge of the scrub to hasten to the filled buckets as quickly as hobbled feet will permit.

Some twenty gallons of water they drink between them. For a little while they stand with legs wide apart, eyes bright, long, split upper-lips waggling. They begin to chew their moistened cuds with vivid enjoyment, content for an hour, but for an hour only, when the desire to return "home" will seize on them.

They have wandered half a mile before they are brought back to the supper prepared for them against the trees to which they are to be tied for the night. Millie is a little vexed at being thus frustrated. Curly is angry and stubborn. Now and then he lies down and bellows like a small child who refuses to walk another yard. Tempers, however, are banished by sight of the prepared supper, when Millie wants to kiss the driver and Curly wants to jump on him.

Routine governs life on the fence. Mental cobwebs cannot be spun. One may take chances with horses or bullocks, but one cannot take chances with camels and long survive. Millie may be trusted a little. Curly may be trusted not to kick with his hind feet and strike with his fore feet, but, when he is being harnessed, his head must be roped close to a tree trunk, and when at work he must not be trusted for a second.

In answer to the oft-put question: "Are you not terribly lonely?" one must answer: "There is no time to be lonely." In one week a fence-rider will read more than the average city man will read over a full year, while his reading will be infinitely more varied. The only part of the life that palls is those windless periods, when for days and nights not a leaf stirs in country where there is but little bird life and no animal life. When the wind is first heard in the distance, roaring across the top of the scrub, one feels inexpressible relief.

Once I had a dog for a companion; but it picked up an old strychnine bait and, despite all efforts, it died in my arms. At another time I took with me a cat that I came to love much, and then Curly stamped on her when she only wanted to rub herself against his dinner-plate foot. I took a young galah. It used to ride all day in the dray and it never knew the bars of a cage. At night, when reading or writing in the dray by the aid of a hurricane lamp, should I be irritated by the visit of a tree moth or a flutter-ing bat, the galah perched on one shoulder would murmur sleepily: "You old devil!" Then one morning, when returning to camp with the camels, I heard a scream of defiance, and, on looking up, was in time to see my bird in the talons of a swiftly-rising hawk.

After that I gave up companions on a rabbit fence. Their loss incurs too much heart-break.

At the 135-mile peg the timber is scattered and the ground is a vast, unbroken carpet of white and gold and blue splashes of colour made by the myriads of wild flowers. Each nodding head is supported on a long stem rising from tiny leaves lying flat on the ground. Weeks after the leaves have perished the flowers remain. In this amazing garden we camp for noon lunch, and while we are eating it in the dray, a bird settles on a fence post to watch us. The world is hushed, and the only sounds are made by the cud-chewing camels and a few blowflies. Presently, at a great distance, one hears belled camels coming our way. The bells grow ever louder exactly as though the camels, or it might be bullocks, are being brought into camp. Done by the entertaining ventriloquist on the post—the bell-bird!

At the 96-mile peg there is a rain-shed and hut combined. Here, in the centre of the great belt of desert bush is an oasis of salt-bush, wait-a-bit, and native peach trees, growing between gnarled red gums. From this splendid camp we go on to the 82-mile peg - where the fence and track passes through a wide gap in a line of break-aways about which the light-ning plays its tricks. A poor camp this. There are many deviations in the fence between this peg and the 69-mile peg from where we turn off into the bush to reach a small hut built in a natural clearing. The clearing is surrounded by wattle trees blazing with heavy, yellow bloom, and the ground on which they grow is snowed deep beneath the white everlasting flowers. A garden, a bush garden, that imperishably burns itself on the mind.

We are in the salmon-gum forest when we pass the 60-mile peg. The tall, straight, lovely trunks of these trees gleam pale against the dark-green background of the lesser bush, and like all gum-trees they shed their bark in preference to their leaves.

We come now to the northern wheat farms in process of creation. The "chop-chop-chop" of biting axes and the whirr of tractors distract us. A mighty heave at the dray, and we are off at a gallop, the rider clinging to the brake-handle protruding from the rear of the vehicle. A settler's wife and children are running through the bush to see their first camels outside a zoo —and the camels are made fearful by the coloured, swaying skirts to which they are quite unaccustomed.

I should glory in Australia's development. Alas, the sound of thudding axes and the splintering crash of falling forest giants both anger and sadden me.

Day by day we pass the endless fence-posts, repair broken wires, and patch the netting torn by the farmers' machines and trucks. In one day we have emerged from the bush proper to the farming districts, where we meet modern road traffic and where it is never silent. We have no place in the world of machinery, this world of cleared spaces not natural to our beloved bush. Perhaps of the three of us, Curly dislikes it least, for it provides him with unlimited excuses to play the fool. At the 25-mile peg we cross the loop railway line at Campion, and thereafter travel nine miles over an established wheat-belt to reach, and pass through, poor ironstone country until, finally, we step on to the main highway from Perth to Kalgoorlie skirting the railway.

The line, of course, breaks the fence; but here it crosses over a deep pit that presents as great a barrier to rabbits as does the fence itself. Beyond the line the mile-pegs begin again at Number One, and across the line we bump and clatter to reach the Government hay farm, where the camels will rest for two days. One mile west lie Burracoppin and the boarding house, where may be eaten fresh yeast bread and butter, celery and red steak for which the body craves after a month's subsistence on tinned food, bacon, and baking-powder bread.

Neither the driver nor the camels are happy here at Burracoppin, and we are emphatically pleased when our faces are again turned northward. Even the desert bush country to us is better than this.

Reaching at last the summit of the rise at the 161-mile, there, falling away from us in a straight line, lies the track to the Camel Station.

The sedate Millie voices her pleasure, and Curly tugs at the trace and wants, oh, so much! to do the last mile and a fraction at express speed.

Down there, where the track appears to be no wider than a small girl's hair ribbon, moves a little black dot. It is the station overseer, who knows the day of our arrival and almost the hour.

How the minutes do drag! We are at the bottom of the slope. Now above the western scrub rise the summits of Dromedary Hill. Then two lonely men are talking like excited women. Five minutes later Curly and Millie are running towards the hill in search of their comrades, free of the wretched hobbles for four days.

Then I am sitting at a real table beneath a house roof. We drink scalding hot tea in the homestead kitchen and shout above the cacophony of two gramophones and the wireless all going at the same time.

They love noise, whose ears have been strained day and night to hear any kind of sound.

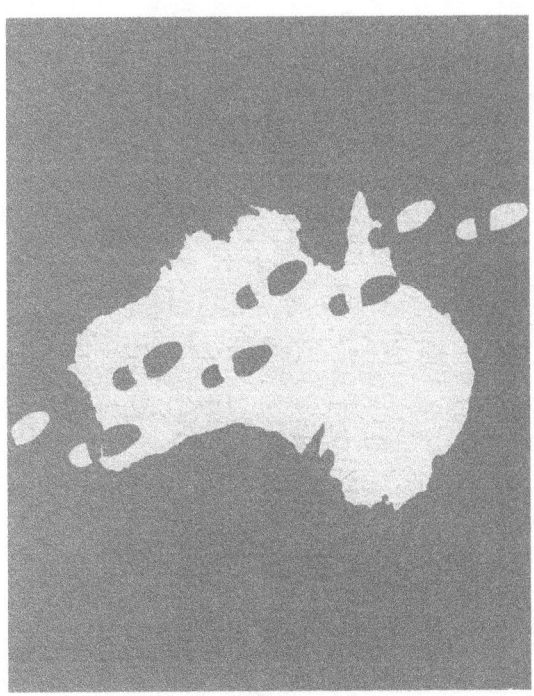

Arthur Upfield's own interpretation of "Walkabout".

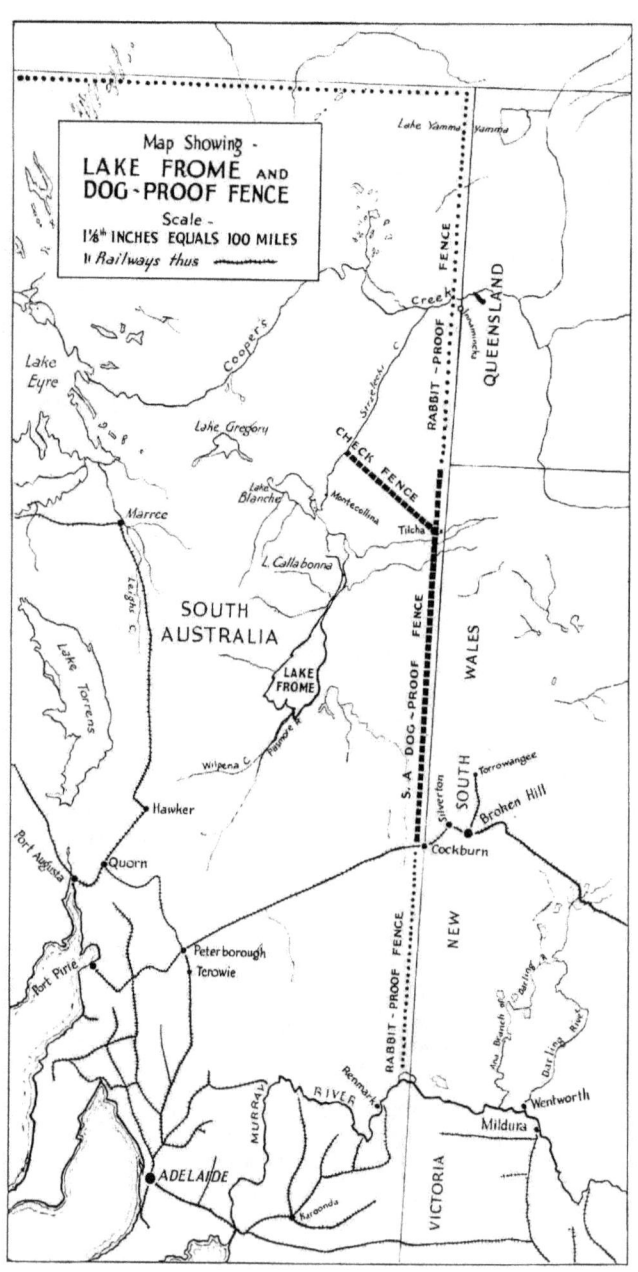

2.

A VISIT TO LAKE FROME

AUSTRALIA's greatest explorer was Sturt. His success was based on cautiousness and foresight and sympathetic care for the members of his party. A perusal of his journals, written during 1844 and 1845, when he left Lake Cawndilla, near Menindee on the Darling, and travelled into the far angle of north-western New South Wales, reveals courage of a high order, born leadership, and the ability calmly to suffer almost unbelievable hardships. The expedition of those years was energized by the belief—based on the stories of the blacks met with during previous expeditions—that to the far north-west lay a great inland sea. The blacks Sturt had previously met had been told of this inland sea by other blacks, whose tribal grounds extended further inland. In actual fact, as Eyre subsequently proved, the inland sea comprised the Lakes Eyre, Torrens, Blanche, and Frome.

Striking off north-westward from Lake Cawndilla, Sturt and his party entered the Barrier Range at not a great distance from where Broken Hill now stands. The season was a dry, one; but, despite this, the explorer slowly worked his way into the very corner of New South Wales, where, beside a shallow depression sometimes holding a little water, he established his farthest north base camp, which he named Fort Grey.

From Broken Hill, the Barrier Range runs approximately due north to merge into another range called the Coko Range. This in turn merges into the Grey Range, which extends far beyond the Queensland border. The hills forming these ranges are low, boulder-strewn, and waterless, and are covered with stunted mulga. Rain-water from them runs to waste over the south-eastern saltbush plains and the north-eastern gibber plains, and into the vast western depression lying beyond the border of South Australia—a veritable wilderness of sand. The hill creeks carry flood water quickly after rain begins to fall; and, very quickly after the rain ceases, they become bone dry. The few springs are hardly worthy of the name.

Into this western wilderness of sand, Sturt led his dauntless companions in summer-time, when the shade heat often is maintained from 100 to 120 degrees night and day for months. Where they hoped and expected to find an inland sea, they discovered an ocean of sandhills.

The South Australian-New South Wales border is marked by an efficiently-guarded, six-feet-high, netted, barb-wire-topped fence. It forms an absolute barrier to the hordes of wild dogs that breed in the vicinity of the desolate mud flats, which, on our maps, are coloured blue and named lakes. The fence, too, bars entry into New South Wales to the extraordinary plagues of rabbits, which, in certain climatic conditions, come out of the barrens in their countless millions.

The upkeep of the fence is undertaken by boundary-riders, who work under the supervision of an overseer. Each man's section is but twenty-two miles in length—and that is twelve miles too long, for they are ever engaged in a terrific battle with the same forces of sand and wind that defeated Sturt.

From the heated interior of the continent spring up strong windstorms, whisking the sand grains high into the air in sufficient density to blot out the sun and, at times, to create pitch-black darkness at noontide. These clouds of sand are often swept eastward as far as Sydney and the coast, and farther still into the Pacific Ocean. Like the tremendous waves of an angry sea, the sandhills under pressure of the westerly gales move with the slowness and the irresistibility of glaciers. The light-red sand of which they are composed is exceedingly fine and will ripple beneath the lightest breeze. One storm will move a sandhill of thousands of tons weight for several yards, burying living trees in its advance and laying bare in its rear trees that have been engulfed for many years.

These ranges of sandhills, each pair divided by a narrow flat, run east-west and seldom at any other angle. By following a flat a car may be driven east or west, but to proceed either north or south would be impossible unless the wheels were replaced by caterpillar traction devices. The country is suitable only for cattle, stock horses, and the camels used by the boundary-riders.

During the months of May, June, and July, the climate is closely allied with that of Egypt in the winter—calm days and cold nights. With September come the fierce wind-storms, two, sometimes three in the week. Occasionally a storm of wind and sand will continue for several days, dying down at night only to regain its violence when the sun rises like a Dutch cheese.

Impelled by the pressure of the wind, countless billions of dead buckbush—balls of straw filigree as large as footballs— roll eastward *en masse*, to be piled against bushes and low scrub trees and the Border Fence until the filigree host is rolled up and over these obstacles to continue the charge. They sweep across the land like a wheat-coloured flood.

Cattle take shelter behind the lee side of trees. Camels will refuse to travel, and they lie down with their hind quarters to the blast, rest their heads on the ground, and pretend to go to sleep. No man born of woman could make them get up and work. On rare occasions a sandstorm will approach without any wind to drive it. At a great distance the wind has dropped to a gentle breeze, and the hot air rising from the ground maintains the sand particles in aerial motion. It will come when the air is motionless, presenting a "face" many miles deep, like a solid brick-red wall threatening to fall upon and destroy the world. Its approach might well terrify the stranger. There is nothing for it but to shelter beneath a tent fly, and to suffer the heat and the lack of air until it has passed on.

Heat and sand and wind and flies during nine months of the year try the most hardened bushman. Save only after heavy rain—quite a phenomenon—there is no surface water. Station people are dependent for drinking water on the catchment from their roofs. Cattle and blacks and fence riders have to subsist on the water provided by the few widely-spaced artesian bores. Without cease, year after year, the bores gush water to form short streams, which vanish among the sand. So loaded with salts is the water forced up the piping from the subterranean depths that the edges of the streams are crusted white with crystals. A much-soiled garment, held on a stick in the steaming water as it gushes from the bore pipe, will require merely to be wrung out after a minute's immersion to become snowy white. Five or six such washings will terminate the usefulness of that garment, for the fibres will have been rotted by the sodas. Tea made with bore water is a failure.

Having travelled west from the Border Fence for some sixty miles, one abruptly emerges from the sandhills to walk down to the shore of Lake Frome. On a clear day it is just possible to discern the red sandhills on the far side. After heavy rain, there might lie on this "lake" two or three inches of water. During the winter and spring it is nothing but a vast mud flat, supporting herbal rubbish and offering a death-trap to venturesome cattle and horses. Across the lake, dingoes form their pads, to seek out the last remaining drops of water in the slight depressions. Encircling the lake are the imprisoning sandhills, with, at the northern end, the gum-trees marking the winding creek coming down from Lake Blanche. It is worse than a desert. A desert is beautiful in its calm death. Here the stunted trees and brittle bush appear to be eternally tormented by the devils in the wind.

Sturt's inland sea! An ocean of wind-tossed, white-capped, green billows! It almost broke Sturt's heart when he had to return from Fort Grey. Had he seen Lake Frome as I saw it one autumn afternoon, I think his heart would have been really broken.

Sheep cross the Tallywalker Creek, photograph by E.V. Whyte.

3.

MEN, SHEEP AND FAR HORIZONS

IF Australia be divided into three geographical zones, there will be revealed striking contrasts between its people and its industries.

Without regard to priority, they are: first, the State Capitals, in which live dense masses of the population, subsisting chiefly on secondary industries; second, the rural districts, extending along the coasts and subdivided into small farms and orchards; and, third, the pastoral lands, which cover almost the whole of the interior of Australia. Each of these zones is producing a distinctive type of human being; this is due far more to environment than to occupation.

Figuratively, the city worker's life is governed by the factory whistle. His face and movements are indicative of the hurly-burly of modern civilization, and between him and the country man and the bushman the gulfs are deep. The farmer and the orchardist, whilst engaged in an incessant battle with Nature to yield her fruits, are cramped by the foreshortened horizons of the farm and the orchard boundaries. On the inland sheep and cattle stations, where the boundaries are as far flung as those of European principalities, the lack of civilization's advantages and amenities is amply compensated by genial labour, more leisure, fewer calls for money, and much more time to read and think. Life is easier. Individual outlook is broader and more tolerant. Freedom is positive.

The average Australian squatter as an employer has no equal in generosity towards his employees. During a quarter of a century's experience of squatters in all States except Tasmania, I have never worked for one who drove his men. It is the rule, not the exception, for the employer never to issue orders twice on the same day; and, when the work allotted has been done, no matter if before mid-day, he will seldom set another task. Some squatters would show annoyance if asked for further work.

The average station-hand reciprocates with a conscientious application to the tasks set him. In no Australian industry is the Arbitration Court's award less necessary than in the pastoral industry; in no other industry are the Court's rulings so flouted by both sides; in no other industry is there to be found such goodwill between master and man; and, in no other industry, is the principle of give and take so well demonstrated.

At one time I was sent to an out-station to cook for two stockmen. They were to arrive the next day. That evening, the "boss" rang up to say they would not be arriving until the end of the week, as he had important work for them to do. For five weeks I did nothing but cook for myself in return for £2/14/8 per week and free food. When, some time after, for a week or so I was obliged to work from dawn till long after dark droving a mob of poor-conditioned sheep, I could discover no right to complain. Taking it by and large, as I have stated, station life is free-and-easy and unique.

It is 7.30 this spring morning at the homestead of a three-quarter-million acre sheep station in western New South Wales. A group of men stand about the large iron building devoted to store-rooms and the office. Above the brilliant green foliage of flanking orange-trees, ranked beyond a white-painted picket fence, mount the red roofs of the "government house"—so named because it houses the station's governing authority. Beyond the large garage are to be seen the men's quarters, and, beyond them, above the straggling box-trees, towers the roof of the great iron shearing-shed, shimmering in the sunlight. Westward grow the giant red-gums, forming the two-thousand-miles-long avenue marking the course of the River Darling.

A party of kookaburras have been roused to demoniacal mirth through the capture of a snake by one of their number. About the killing pens the crows are quarrelling. The galahs, who at dawn welcomed the new day with peace-shattering cacophony, have departed for their feeding grounds, far out over the river flats.

Through the gate in the picket fence comes the boss. His face and hands are tanned by wind and sun, and the manner in which he walks with his toes slightly inward proclaims the many years he has lived on the back of a horse.

"Morning," he says, when drawing near the waiting men.

"Morning, Mr. Smith. Morning."

Absently, the squatter scratches his head. He frowns with seeming perplexity. The stranger would think that the bane of his life was finding work for many more hands than he needed. Then:

"I want you to pump water to-day, Tom."

Nodding assent, old Tom departs for the powerful steam engine on the river bank below the reservoir tanks set high on a staging. From them water is piped to all points, as well as to the garden, an oasis in what a visitor would regard as a semi-desert.

"Ned, I want you to go out to Half-Circle Creek, and pull all the wire from that old fence. I was out there yesterday. The wire is still quite good. Coil it neatly, and stack it behind the poison house. Take the dray and Nugget. Harry, have a look at the fences in Ryde's Well. Fred, you and Alec go along to Deep Bend and have a look at the rams. Have a look at Boggy Corner. We might have to fence it off later. Arthur, I am going outback. I'll want you with me. We'll be away a couple of days."

Departing as our orders are received, we leave the boss talking with the blacksmith until the house gong calls him to breakfast. The horses come galloping from the night paddock: behind the cloud of dust raised by their thudding hoofs stutters like a machine-gun the groom's stockwhip. The fencer and the stock- men saunter to the men's kitchen to cut their noon lunch. Old Tom makes for the pumping engine's separate wood-heap. To-day I shall want only my swag. My lunch will come out of the boss's well-packed hamper.

While he is at breakfast, the car is got out and the tank and the radiator are filled. A case of petrol has to go into the tonneau with the tucker-box and the swags, and, from the homestead cook, the delectable hamper. The bookkeeper hurries from the office with the mail for the out-station, and for the two huts we shall pass before reaching it.

It is 9 o'clock when we leave the river, speeding across the three-miles-wide, grey flats, dotted with box-trees and long since made barren by the rabbit plagues that swept down from the north in the 'nineties.

There is the first gate to open before reaching the far edge of the flats. The track rises gently to worm its way into a belt of big timber, the rise forming a bank of the river when one of the great floods comes sliding' down from the watersheds of Southern Queensland.

We pass solitary, gnarled, and unlovely swamp gums—the favourite nesting trees of the galahs—box-trees, the yellow- flowering native tobacco bushes, and grand old man saltbush. Patches of grey sand intermingle with patches of spear-grass. Clay-pans and shallow water-gutters prove that, even here, the floods have passed, widening the river to ten, twenty miles.

Abruptly the car slips down to the edge, of a plain, on which grows lush herbage: the juicy buckbush, the cotton-bush, the annual saltbush, and the waving, ripening grasses. The sky is a bowl, blue-varnished, sweeping down to the timber ahead, elongated by the mirage to the likeness of Eastern date-palms; its rim resting on the humps of distant sand-hills to the south, and made jagged by the long sand-ridge running eastward on our left.

Another gate to stop us! Another gate to open, and to close when the car has passed through. In 20 minutes we have crossed the plain, and are following the track in among the box-trees that mask the maze of channels skirting the Tallywalker Creek. In and out, down and across, the track chooses the easiest way and the hardest surface. The ground appears to open when we reach the main creek, revealing a narrow strip of water, muddy, defiant of the sun to tinge it with colour. Grey, red-legged, red-billed Queensland ducks waddle down the far steep bank to join a party of black mountain ducks unconcernedly paddling among quaint, huge-billed pelicans.

Passing over a natural ford in the Tallywalker, the track rises sharply to a small clearing, covered by the low, ghostly plants whose seeds are protected by a covering of iron-hard wood, from which protrude long, fine spikes—the Three-cornered Jacks, so beloved by the galahs. Beyond the flat, above a low, bush- covered sand-ridge, is seen the upper portion of a pine-built hut. A dog races to welcome us. Stopping at the door, the cook of the mustering camp rolls out to stand beside the car. Three cats follow him to rub themselves against his legs.

"Morning, Bill."

"Mornin', Mr. Smith. Got time for a cupper tea?"

"No, not now, thanks. There is some mail here for your lads. The water in the lagoon's drying up. Soon be gone. Last another fortnight, perhaps. Mr. Black down at the yards?"

"Yes. They got the sheep in late last night."

A flock of Major Mitchell' cockatoos flies overhead, splashes of pink and white against the blue of the sky, a dream of colour shattered by defiant screeches. We leave the cook regretfully gazing after us, the cats still controlled by cupboard love.

Over a bar of golden sand runs the track, deep twin ruts made by motor traffic—lines the car must follow as a train must follow the iron rails. Crossing another dry creek, another wide clearing, we round a spur of timber to reach the maze of yards named, from the timber constructing them, Pine Yards.

Up from them grey dust rising; in them blurred figures of men labouring in the dust, black and red dogs flashing over the low division fences. Men ya-ho-dilling. Dogs frantically barking. Sheep milling, sheep churning, sheep running like lime-wash down a gutter, sheep complaining to high heaven in one continuous bleat. We climb though the outer wire fence, then over two pine-log division fences to reach the side of the overseer as he works a gate giving entry to three small yards. His eagle eye distinguishes the ear-marks of the sheep streaming through the race towards him. Here a calm, placid ewe travelling a road she knows well; now a matron, who looks as though she would like to give us a piece of her mind; now a pert wench full of conceit. Each animal has its distinct personality; all have in their veins the blue blood of the aristocratic merino of Ancient Spain.

The sheep on this run, numbering 55,000, are being finally drafted for the year. The raddle marks are still freshly brilliant on their machine-shortened wool. For weeks they have been driven by men and dogs, handled and drafted, and now before them are long months of peace and security and content.

We leave the sheepmen to run across the flat and around a headland of light-red sand. Eastward then to skirt sand-dunes presenting a rugged coast to the sea of the vast northern plain, limited on its far side by the dark, hair-like line of scrub. We follow the "beach" of claypans, as hard as cement, as level as a billiard table. Out at "sea" flutters a flock of big, black birds resembling crows. The sluggish manner in which they take to wing, as well as their raucous cries, proclaims them to be black, scarlet-under-winged cockatoos.

Ahead, at the foot of the towering sandhills, a grey post resolves itself into a kangaroo, white-waistcoated, grey-backed. Presently, as one, nine others spring up to watch the oncoming car. A moment—two, perhaps—they stare, bodies motionless. The leader then crouches, moves forward like a swimmer diving from a low board. Unhurriedly he hops and hops out on to the plain, followed as unhurriedly by the others. Far away feed a flock of sheep, white dots dropped carelessly on Nature's immense grey-green carpet.

Having followed the "coast" for four miles, having left the homestead sixteen miles behind, the track takes a sharp turn to the south to enter a narrow-mouthed bay. To the right we pass a surface dam, its dirty-white banks of mullock rising above a base of lantana. On the left we pass the fire-blackened remains of an old hut. Here is Burnt Hut Tank. Again the track turns eastward, now to slip upward between two mountains of sand, in colour that of Australian gold. They are the gateposts to a land of low sand-dunes, the ridges naked, the lower slopes supporting ripening grasses, the dividing gullies giving root to the hardy mulgas, the sombre pines, and the graceful sandalwoods. A tall, shapely leopard-wood-tree beckons us.

From the shade cast by a pine-tree, two emus dash on to the track to pilot us. The emu is considered to be the world's fastest running creature, and these two prime specimens are timed by the speedometer. The pointer moves upwards from 30 to 40 miles an hour. Sand flung high by twinkling feet lashes the wind-screen like storm rain. Forty-three miles an hour is registered before the birds show signs of fatigue. The speed is quickly reduced to a mere 10 miles an hour, and then, as abruptly as they had dashed on to the track, they leave it to disappear into the unwinding scrub.

"Once I chased an emu at 46 miles to the hour," the Boss remarks. "That was a record."

Blue-bush gleams like steel in the sunlight. Saltbush lies like grey velvet patches on earth's brown and green garments. Tussock-grass waves in the gentle wind like ripening corn. The glinting spear-grass looks like the points of assegais carried by Zulus.

The sand-dunes open before us, breaking back to present us with a vision of space opening before us like a woman's fan unfolding. We glide down a gradient into a maze of sand-hillocks and water-gutters. The fierce westerlies coming after rain have fashioned the hillocks with the hands of a master into tall, slender columns, feminine figures clothed in hobble skirts, realistic images of reptilian monsters, churches and arches. The ground slopes away southward to the feet of giant sand-hills— treeless, grassless, barren. Here is a hell of dust and whistling shrieks when the westerlies blow.

After travelling 26 miles, we reach two huts and a windmill set on high land above a swamp that now is dry. Wheeler's Well they call it, after the contractor who sank the well. Finding no one at home, the two stockmen being out somewhere on the run, we leave the mail on the kitchen table. Three miles farther on we pass an unused hut, and, after another half-mile, we stop for lunch beside two huge reservoir tanks flanking a windmill; from them projects a hundred yards of water troughing. At the close of one dry and hot summer an exiled Frenchman came this way. It was before the well was put down. If only he could have obtained half a pint of the water, which runs 75 feet underground, he would not have perished.

Here, at the Frenchman, while the billy boils the boss inspects the tanks and the mill. I take a stroll along the low iron troughing, noting that the sheep in this paddock have not been to drink since the day before—over their tracks are the tracks of foxes, and they leave their rabbit warrens only at night.

We eat daintily-cut sandwiches and drink from tin pannikins. We talk of sheep and wild dogs and the price of wool. We discuss books and bullocks, and the poor Frenchman who died here.

And then our purring ship steams out across another and a larger plain. The scrub sinks behind us, drawing downward into a dark line. On the southern horizon, a single sand-hill juts above the earth like a woman's finger-nail. Ahead rises the first of many swells. It is fully 12 miles across this plain of spear-grass and annual saltbush, and small swamps heavy with pigweed, the whole forming the station's best paddock. When other paddocks are Saharas beneath the scrub trees, this maintains in good condition as many sheep as during normal seasons.

Looking back, one may see to the north-west a knife-edged mass of cloud. Rain! Nearly all our rain comes from that quarter. The car hums along over the rises and down into the declivities. At last the plain is crossed; we have gained the far scrub-lined shore. Here we pass through another gate, turn sharply to the right, and run down a rough track to a well and drinking troughs named, after the great dry lake, Ratcatcher.

From the mill-head one gazes across a ribbon of sand-ridges to the wide-flung land depression which, since the white man snagged the Darling, has never held water. It is the southern link of a chain of beautiful lakes, which, when Nature banked back the water of the river, were kept filled by a narrow and shallow creek running from the river above Wilcannia. Among the sand-drifts, between dry lake and mill, to-day may be found the bones and the skulls of the slain in a fierce aboriginal battle. Among the drifts, too, may be found the flat nardoo stones on which the women pounded seeds to flour, mute representatives of tribal peace and plenty. At points around the lake's shore remain great heaps of the shells of the mussels collected by the natives when this land was softened and beautified by sheets of permanent water.

Again on the main track! Dust ahead! We catch up with a mob of travelling sheep in charge of two stockmen. They are moving parallel with the road; and, when we stop, one of the horsemen canters across to us. Big, black eyes gleam with the joy of living. A big, round black face beams down at us as though we were near and dear relatives. The descendant of that tribe, perhaps, who defended so valiantly their camping ground beside Lake Ratcatcher, this 1934 aboriginal wears polished elastic-sided riding boots, white moleskin trousers, a khaki shirt, and a wide-brimmed felt hat. On one finger glitters a diamond ring; between his teeth is clamped the stem of a silver-mounted pipe.

"How are the sheep travelling, Pinto?"

"Good-oh, boss. We put 'em into Waterloo paddock, eh?"

"That's right. Don't hurry them. You have plenty of time to get them there before sundown. Going to rain?"

"'Spect so. Hope so. Plenty grass then."

"There will be. Who owns that yellow dog?"

"I do."

"Splash of cattle dog about him. Bite?"

"Nope." The stockman laughed with genuine humour. "If he bite the sheep, I'll boot the stuffin' out of him. I will so."

"Humph! See that he doesn't. Good-bye."

"Good-bye, boss."

On again for mile after mile, across undulating country bearing only here and there small clusters of belars and single pines, and swathed with vast areas of ripening grass. Up and up a long rise. Presently the summit is reached, and low in the near distance, like a bud breaking into a gorgeous bloom, there bursts upon our eyes an oval sheet of lapis lazuli. Water! Victoria Lake—2 miles across and 3 miles long. The year before, the water was 15 feet deep. In another year it will have vanished—sucked up by the sun and wind at the rate of 5 feet per annum. Twenty-one years that lake was dry. It may be dry for another period of twenty years.

The sun darkens, vanishes. The shadow speeds faster than the car. We can watch it, eating up the brick-red land, passing with the swiftness of a bird's shadow over the red roofs of the out-station, built beside the water. It moves in a rule-straight line across the lake, breathing from the water its sun-created colours.

We have this day covered 50 miles. The boss says we will have to visit the back boundary of the run to-morrow. That will mean another 30 miles, for the run is 80 miles in length. At this out-station live men whom I have not seen for months.

Two fishermen who net and take to Broken Hill—125 miles to the west—a ton of fish every week, sit in the men's quarters after dinner and gossip with us. For an hour the conversation is kept to the question of spiritual survival after death; and Haeckel, Doyle and Lodge are mentioned as authorities. The subject gives place to the chances of such-and-such a horse at the next important race meeting.

"Come on, you fellers! What about a little game of poker?"

It is raining softly, steadily. From out the darkness comes the incessant chatter of the water-birds on the lake. The tame galah, perching on one of the roof beams, replies to the gambler.

"What a day! What a day!" it murmurs sleepily.

Wool classer DL Fitzgerald at Albermarle Station during Upfield's time there, photographed by E.V. Whyte.

4.

HOSTS HIDDEN IN THE BUSH

MANY visitors to the Australian bush have been disappointed by the apparent scarcity of its wild life. Surprise is expressed when no glimpse of kangaroo or emu is obtained, and when miles of country are crossed without a sight of Australia's world-famed sheep.

There are several reasons for this apparent scarcity of wild life, both indigenous and foreign, in comparison with other countries of like size and development. In order of importance the chief of these reasons are: the vast extent of land undivided by great mountain ranges, broad rivers, and real deserts; the fact that drought is never universal but always local in scope, so that there are many wide districts enjoying bounteous seasons when other districts are less favoured ; and, thirdly, that the visitor usually selects the winter or the spring for his tour, when countless lagoons and swamps and claypans are filled with water.

It is during the middle and the late summer months, and all the natural water catchments are dried up, when all the beasts and the birds converge to man-made water supplies, that their variety and numbers may be appreciated. The necessity to drink brings all living things from timid concealment in the bush into the open—which is to say, all birds and beasts.

Let us spend a full day at Twin Wells in the north-west of New South Wales, and let the day selected be in February.

The two wells are sunk only fifty yards apart; yet one contains fresh water at a depth of eighty-five feet, and the other has water more heavily laden with salt than is the sea. Above each well are erected a windmill and an auxiliary petrol pumping-engine, and, so great is the demand for water by the daily visitors, each well has to contribute fifty per cent. of the water raised and piped into a set of large iron receiving tanks, from which it is piped in turn to two long lengths of troughing.

Twin Wells is situated in the centre of an unnatural plain having a radius of one mile. The plain is just a disk of red-brown sand amidst the encircling scrub; a disk created by the stock and the wild things that, summer after summer, congregate about the source of the life-maintaining water; a disk long since denuded of herbage and scrub trees, and very early this particular summer it had been made bare of grass by the animals constantly travelling across it.

Day having won temporary victory over Night, the clear and dry atmosphere increases vision to the extent of enabling one to distinguish the trunks of individual trees growing at the edge of the scrub a full mile distant. In the hessian-built lean-to beside one of the receiving tanks, the thermometer registers 88°, the lowest figure yet reached since the dawn of yesterday. Immediately the sun appears, the mercury begins to mount, and by seven o'clock it has reached the 100 mark.

Several crows, their cunning forgotten in the desire to drink, settle on the edges of the troughs without any preliminary scouting to ascertain the presence of possible enemies. During the period of twenty minutes, half-a-dozen small flocks of galahs —rose-breasted, grey-backed parrots—arrive to drink with even greater haste than that exhibited by the crows.

At eight o'clock, when the thermometer registers 108°, there is not a single bird to be seen, bar two wedge-tailed eagles flying so high as to appear no larger than flies. Nowhere on the plain is to be seen any living creature. The sun haze has resolved into a shimmering lake by, nine o'clock and, as the hot minutes pass, the "lake" becomes split up into pools and lagoons, beyond which the distorted scrub is magnified into tall palms standing in water.

The mounting mercury has just passed the 114° mark at ten o'clock when the first of the wandering "whirlies," attenuated and faint of colour, marches out of the scrub on to the plain, which gives it material for growth and freedom for action. The plain sand is seen whirling upward into the wind vortex, high and higher, until a massive, thousand-feet high, brick-red column rushes across the open spaces with roaring triumph.

These whirlies create the only sound in an otherwise soundless world.

The air beyond their sphere of action is utterly without motion. The baked earth radiates sun-stored heat, whilst the rays of the sun on exposed iron make it unbearable to touch. At eleven o'clock the thermometer registers 118° of heat—in the shade—and an hour later two further degrees are added.

Shortly after noon, shadows dance above the mirage pools.

Still other shadows appear to be wafted between the sheets of spurious water. They take on the substance of living things, and presently emerge to human vision like over-dressed old ladies walking on stilts. Gradually the stilts disappear, and long, graceful necks come into being, and there is seen the stately "ostrich" of Australia. Through the mirage stalk the emus, hundreds of them, to take their daily, drink at noon, beaks wide open and throat feathers throbbing. Exhibiting no nervousness and without unmannerly haste, they approach the troughs, where some drink standing, and others lie down to drink.

The observer need not trouble to hide himself from, these birds. If he remains seated arid exercises a little patience, they will draw so close to him that he could toss a pebble to them. Should he sit down in open country where emus are feeding, and wave his handkerchief continuously, they will gather about him – this time controlled by curiosity.

By two o'clock they have all vanished beyond the mirage, gone to stand in the shade of the scrub trees, which shelter countless, animals that pant in the heat and wait for the evening to arrive, when they may dare the trek to the water.

Even the jaws of the domestic cat are wide open as she lies gasping, although sheltered from the sun at the side of a receiving tank. Cats hate water! This one will stand whilst cool water from the canvas drinking bag is poured over her, and will gratefully lie down in a shallow-scooped hole after water is poured into it.

Unable longer to endure the torture of thirst, a foolish crow has left the scrub and is to be seen flying erratically towards the well. Attention is attracted to it by the unusual notes of its cawing. On it comes, as though it were drunk, and then, when within a hundred yards of its goal, it abruptly, folds its wings and "nose dives," to crash to the plain in a little cloud of dust —smitten dead by the sun it has defied.

The afternoon's silence is shattered by the thudding petrol-engines and the whine of pumps; for, before the hosts of evening visitors arrive, all the receiving tanks must be brim full. For many days there has been no wind strong enough to drive the windmills.

Silence reigns again when the sun, turned blood-red by the, heat haze and promising faithfully another hot day on the morrow, draws down to the scrub and seems to dissipate the mirage lake. Then small black dots are observed at the edge of the scrub, jumping like common fleas. There are hundreds of these jumpers, spaced along the full circle of scrub, and presently little spurts of dust rise at each landing when the "flea" have, grown into bounding balls progressing to the wells. As though machine-gun bullets are being fired from the wells to ricochet across the surface of the plain, the dust spurts rise much higher than each "ball" at the apex of the jumps. In less than a minute the foremost creatures are within two hundred yards of the troughs, when they resolve into the graceful, noble, and community-loving kangaroos. There they sit as motionless as the carved gods of savage tribes, longing to reach the water but not daring to come closer without the protection of the night.

Behind these continue to come others, and then one's attention is caught and held by a rising cloud of red dust beyond the edge of the scrub to the north.

High and higher rises the cloud to become a gigantic column stained crimson by the setting sun. Slowly it draws near and nearer to the plain; no whirlie, this, no roaring tumult of heated air rushing upward as through a funnel to the cool high altitudes.

The sun, touching the scrub, seems to fire it. The great dust column has now reached the edge of the plain and beneath it appear dull-white splashes crawling across the ground. Dense masses of heat-lifted sand swirl upward to darken still more redly the advancing column, sand churned and energized by the hooves of seven thousand sheep marching in parallel lines.

From out of the turquoise eastern sky drop flighting redbreasts— smaller than the English robin and much more vividly painted in scarlet and in black. For a little while they flit above the open receiving tanks, drinking on the wing, and then are gone as silently as they came.

Soft, whispering, child-like voices first announce the coming of the combined flocks of all the galahs in this district. They come in a mighty host that breaks into divisions on arrival: one division to alight on the rails of stock trap-yards; another to settle on the ground beyond the end of one of the troughs; other divisions to settle on the ground at different places like grey blankets now that their rose-coloured breasts are not in such evidence.

The waiting kangaroos rarely move. The sheep are coming across the plain at steady pace, only their leaders being visible, as though they are carrying the dust column on their backs. Far away, other 'roos are leaving the scrub and, although they cannot be seen, the vanguard of the army of rabbits is well on the way.

All about the wells and the troughs, the galahs are flying in disorganized units. The edges of both troughs are painted grey by them. Th e close-pressing birds are lowering and raising their pink-crested heads like mechanical birds in a toy shop. The peace of the evening is shattered by their discordant cries.

The leaders of the sheep flock are rearing the troughs. The mass of red dust rising straight from them threatens to fall forward and bury the wells and the plain. They come, those leaders, at an ever quickening pace, pursued by the muffled murmur of their thirst-tormented followers. They are no chance leaders appointed for the day, and they are led by one commander-in-chief, a wise old ewe. She is leading her line much ahead of the sub-leaders and their lines, and thus she has led the flock for several months.

The kangaroos hop to either side to give passage to the sheep. From the dust column comes a continuous baaing of impatient animals, punctuated by deep-chested coughs. With a low rumble of hooves, the lines reach the water troughs, and the drinking birds rise as one with screaming protest.

Outward from the troughs spreads the flow of wool. The column of dust becomes stationary, seemingly supported by the straining, pushing, complaining mass of sheep. The water begins rapidly to sink in the troughs, and the ball-valves hiss as the water gushes from the receiving tanks.

The sheep leader, having distended her flanks with water, turns and butts her way out of the press. Clear of it, she walks slowly to a point about one hundred yards away, and there halts to chew her cud and now and then glance back at her milling comrades. Others, also water-laden, walk out to take position behind her, never in front of or beside her, and thus she and they stand until every sheep has drunk its fill and is waiting to move off.

The dust subsides for a little while. About the troughs the galahs wheel and wheel, laying streaks of scarlet and of grey across the azure canvas of the sky. Continuously they scream at one another and mockingly shriek at the crows.

The kangaroos come in a little closer, wary yet. The galahs are gathering on the ground preparatory to departure. The sheep begin to move away, and again there rises the great column of red dust. An oncoming rabbit from which caution, cunning, even fear have been banished by the awful determination to reach the water, enters the close-packed ranks of the birds. They rise into the air as one bird and, as one bird, they wheel to the south and depart with screams of defiance.

The western sky is like the wall of a slaughter-house. The tips of the miniature sandhills thrown up by the trampling hooves are stained scarlet by the afterglow. Across the crimson-flecked ground come quick-moving, brown shadows—the rabbits.

The western glow is fading. The steel-blue edge of the indigo dome of night is pressing it downward to the sharply silhouetted horizon.

The rabbits begin to gather beneath the troughs where the water drips between the iron plates. Sitting up on their haunches, they are licking the forming drops. Others jump up on the troughs' side rails and, crouching forward, drink like cats. Sentinel kangaroos spring up and bring down their tails in warning "thrumps" when the more venturesome begin to move toward the water on all fours, creeping soundlessly like spider creatures from a Wellsian world.

The day has almost vanished. The mercury has dropped to a cool 101°. A zephyr of air comes from the north-east. A belated crow arrives to flutter above the wells and to caw mournfully. Barely visible against the dark sky, it flies off to some tree in which to roost, wracked by thirst till the dawning.

Soft, slithering noises made by the converging host of rabbits, inter-rupted by the loud warning of sentinel kangaroos, fill the night. A flash-light reveals a mass of animals along each side of both troughs into which the ball valves permit the life-saving water to gush and gush. There comes a low rumble of furred feet when the rabbits dash aside to give passage-way to a fox that begins to lap-lap-lap like a dog as though it never will stop drinking. A rabbit screams, and the flashlight shows it being carried off in the jaws of a fox that turns its head and reveals the green fire of its eyes.

Save for the emus, all the day has been empty, and silent. Now, during the first half of the night, life surges around Twin Wells, life that would perish in forty-eight hours were the ball valves to be fixed and permit no water to pass.

Dawn reveals no living thing other than the crows. The tracks made by the sheep on the sandy ground have been obliterated by the feet of rabbits, and the pads of foxes and of kangaroos, and of one wild dog.

Should thunderstorms let fall a deluge of water before the setting of the sun, Twin Wells will be deserted until the natural catchments again dry up; but day after day the burnished sky remains empty of clouds, and day after day the mercury in the thermometer mounts in its glass tube to the 120 mark.

E.V. Whyte (left) and friends, droving sheep from New South Wales into Queensland.

Tom Cole, who began by driving cattle from Queensland to the Territory, is perhaps more celebrated as a buffalo hunter, seen here in 1932.

5.

COMING DOWN WITH CATTLE

THE great cattle stations, situated inland beyond the sheep runs, send outward their streams of living beasts through three main channels, created by the dictates of seaboard cities and the harbours from which thousands of tons of beef annually are exported across the world. The genesis of one of these channels is on the vast tablelands of the Northern Territory, and it conducts cattle to the railheads at Longreach, Winton, and Charleville with which to supply the demands of Brisbane and Sydney. The second channel begins on that country drained by the Strzelecki, Barcoo, and Cooper's Creeks in the North-east of South Australia, the far South-west of Queensland, and the far North-west of New South Wales. Running southward to Cockburn and the railway, it supplies the Melbourne and Adelaide markets. A third stream, starting from the Kimberleys of Western Australia and the North-west of the

Territory, ends at the Wyndham meat-works, which operate throughout the winter months.

Not all the cattle on the track, however, are destined for immediate consumption. Having followed one of the main channels or stock routes, many beasts find resting and fattening quarters on the small selections and the large farms lying along the rim of the pastoral country proper. From these farms they can be rushed quickly by rail to a city market when in top condition. Fattening store cattle is quite an industry, and distinct from cattle-rearing. The men engaged in this industry may well be termed cattle-farmers, who buy cattle on the hoof to fatten; and by far the greater proportion of beef bought in butchers' shops comes from these farms after having been reared on distant cattle stations.

His mob of steers slowly approaching the wide boundary gate of a South-western Queensland station has begun a 700-mile long journey to Adelaide. At this time in Adelaide the price is "right." It is likely to remain right for several months. The seasons have been kinder to the North than to the South; and, consequently, these cattle are well-conditioned when fat cattle down around the city are scarce. Should the drover exercise ordinary ability, they should reach the butchers without loss of condition.

Seated on their horses outside the fence and close to the open gate are the manager and the boss drover. Farther back, near to a patch of belars, are grouped the drover's men and the cook's wagonette. They await a sign from their leader to carry on, when the station men have put the cattle through the gate, and when the "hand-over" has been completed. It is seldom that station cattlemen drove their own cattle.

The close-pressed lines of moving steers form the base of a dust, column slowly rising to the cloudless sky. A horseman shoots out from the edge of the column to race forward and take position to force the leaders of the mob more directly to the gate. Behind the column of dust come occasional whip- cracks, soft-pedalled by the low moan of complaining beasts.

"How are you on tallying?" asks the manager, who is no better dressed than the drover and his men.

On the drover's brick-red face grows a twisted smile.

"Me—I generally gets to within fifty or so," he replies.

The cattle come on steadily. There are no rushes, no halting, no hesitation. They begin to pour through the gate like sand grains through an hour glass, and presently two of the drover's men ride out wide to persuade the beasts that have passed through to mill quietly until the hand-over is completed. The two men by the gate keenly watch the passing animals swirling between the stout posts in twos and threes and fives. Then, when all have passed by:

"Well?" inquires the manager.

"Nine hundred and forty-one," is the confident answer.

"Correct. Get 'em to Cockburn on November 22nd, remember. So long, and good hunting."

"Ta-ta! See you some more."

The drover nods his farewell and wheels his horse to follow the cattle. The action is the signal to his men that the tally has been decided. With crackling whips they begin to get the cattle out of the mill, then to force them on down the southward track. The boss drover jogs along to catch up with them; the manager rides his hack through the gate, closes it without dismounting, and canters after his men, who have turned back to the homestead.

The cattle are on the move! The dust column continues its steady southward march. Well forward on either flank rides a horseman. To the rear of each flank rides another. Behind the mob docilely walk the night horses in charge of the tailer, whose work is to "boss" all the horses in the outfit. He rides with one leg twisted across the saddle pommel to gain a change of position. His jaws are ever at work, chewing tobacco. They are even thus engaged when he rides an outlaw horse for amusement. Far to the left the cook, driving his two-horse wagonette, is going on to prepare the night camp.

"Full count, Tim?" drawls the tailer.

"Nine short of nine-fifty. Ain't a bad lookin' lot."

"Nope. Better'n I expected. Oughter average eight hundred pounds dressed." Emphatically he waved away the cloud of small flies hovering about his head. "Can you tell me why I go drovin'?" he asks plaintively.

For a while they ride together. Then, when two steers fall out to engage in combat, the boss drover canters forward to snap his long whip on their rumps.

The cattle are quiet, unsuspicious. They are still on their own country. For the first time this day they are free of the tormenting horsemen who insisted on cutting out from among them those beasts not up to general standard. At long last they are free to appease their hunger with speargrass and cotton bush. The weather is cool and the day windless. The uninitiated would have thought that drovers led easy and delightful lives.

The days are cool and clear. The nights are still and cold. Across the plains move the beasts, strung out into long lines, feeding whilst they walk; through the mulga belts to snap and tear at the lower branches; and so to the grey flats bordering Cooper's Creek.

With sheep may be taken rolls of hessian and light stakes with which to erect a temporary yard for the night. With cattle no material can be taken that will hold them. From the day they leave their familiar station country until they are trucked at a railhead, drovers have to wage constant battle with refractory beasts whose behaviour cannot be estimated one minute ahead.

Having travelled all day, having eaten its fill and drunk its fill at a creek or a bore stream, an animal might be expected to lie down peacefully for the night. Not so a steer on track. During the first two weeks it ever wants to break back to the paddock wherein it first saw the light, whilst always it wants to be badly frightened, and will ever seek excuses for becoming so.

Westward moves the mob along the gum-lined Cooper's Creek, passing by Oontoo to reach the Queensland-South Australia Rabbit Fence. The season further westward has been good, and reports have it that water lies in the deep holes along the bed of the Strzelecki. Before reaching the township of Innamincka we leave the Cooper's to strike south-westward to join the Strzelecki, then to follow this creek southward. To avoid the fenced stations of Carraweena and Monte-Collina, we leave the Strzelecki Creek sixty miles down its course to strike off through the barrens to Tilcha Station opposite the Northwest corner of New South Wales. Thus, not a single fence hinders our passage from Innamincka to Tilcha, almost one hundred miles. Here lie ranges of sand and wide belts of dense mulga and gibber plains. It is a country impassable in dry seasons a no-man's land. Here is the country known by Sturt and by the ill-fated Burke and Wills; here are no motor tracks, nor even wagon tracks, and the aeroplane has yet to fly overhead.

South of Tilcha, we follow the South Australian-New South Wales Dog-proof Fence across an endless succession of sand ridges, extending from beyond the fence to the shores of Lake Frome.

All day long we ride on the flanks or behind the mob. For hours one just rides and smokes. Sometimes, in fierce bursts of energy, we have to deal with animals that have the very devil in them. A wall-eyed black-and-white steer gives more trouble than a hundred others, and, were all like a certain broad- backed Hereford, the night would be worth sleeping through. As it is, just when you have fallen asleep, rough hands shake you, and a gruff voice says:

"Come on! Get out! It's your turn to do a bit of yo-ho-dilling." Then it is to roll from beneath your blankets, pull on elastic-side boots, and lurch to the coffee billy standing beside the great camp fire. Your duty mate joins you, and over a pannikin of hot coffee you roll a cigarette and listen to the restless murmur of discontented beasts. You think of the station hands luxuriating in warm bunks, and you wonder why you ever went a-droving. That black and white steer will be sure to start trouble during your watch.

Your night horse is waiting, left for you by the man who roused you out. It stands on the firelight's border, quiet but keenly intelligent, anchored to the ground by the reins falling from the bridle.

The stars gleam unsympathetically. Semi-stunned by the want of sleep, you clamber aboard your horse like a sailor on leave, when, without orders or guidance, it walks smartly to the night-enshrouded cattle. You begin to whistle or to sing, wanting to do neither the one nor the other. Your mate has gone the other way. You hear him singing "The Face on the Bar-room Floor." Heavens ! Isn't there a more cheerful tune and song than that for such an occasion?

Out of the midnight pall first comes a *sense* of motion. Then can be seen motion, but precisely what would be impossible to distinguish were it not for the moan and stress of bovine minds. There they are—nearly a thousand beasts. You sing anything, and you whistle anything, just to make a familiar noise to let those suspicious minds know it is only you. Confound it! Why cannot they camp like other animals and the birds? It will be that black-and-white steer again making off for home, and leading a string of rebels. Your horse sees the attempted breakaway. Before you can direct him, he is taking you at a canter to head them off, to turn them back into the mob. You can hear your mate singing away on the far side, and you fervently hope that should the mob stampede they will not come your way.

Cattle will stampede for any reason, and for no reason at all. A screaming curlew, a snapped twig, even a match being struck will bring to their feet all beasts lying down. Quicker than fire spreads over spilt petrol, mass panic will ignite every bovine brain. A huge, featureless shape might roll towards you like lava, having in its unleashed power the destruction of lava. You remember all the advice previously given relative to such a situation, and your horse is as ready to act on it as you are.

You are carried along through the black night at express speed. Behind, thunder merciless hooves. Behind, a hissing, crashing, dreadful uproar. Terrified by the possibility of your horse falling, or of your being swept off his back by a tree branch to go down beneath the following avalanche, all you can do is to lie along your horse's neck and wildly pray "Trust your horse" is the advice of the old-timers. It is good advice, too, if your horse is an experienced stock horse, but less good if he is not experienced. He can see the ground and the trees that are invisible to you. He will take a wide curve, and the terror behind will thus draw to one side, finally to move away, to leave you well bushed, because you have paused not to note direction.

After a week or two on the track, cattle will begin to settle down. Becoming a little used to the changed conditions, they will, like human beings fully employed, be glad enough to enjoy the leisure of the long nights. To the cattleman track life has its compensations and much charm. His appetite for changing scenes is kept blunted. Mostly by day he rides alone, keeping his station. At night he rides alone, too. He becomes weather- wise and cattle-wise. His repertoire of songs is amazing, whilst many there are whose whistling ability would be an asset on any stage.

When the long day is drawing to a close, when half the journey is done, when the cattle have been streaming over the sand-ridges and across the dividing flats of this amazing Lake Frome Dog-proof Fence country, sight of the cook's wagonette and the rising smoke of the camp fire is always gladsome. Having drunk at the stream that has its beginning at an everlastingly gushing bore-head, the cattle are ready to lie down and chew their cuds whilst the twilight deepens. We remove the harness from weary horses, and permit them to roll in the light-brown sand before strapping on the hobbles. The night horses are held in readiness for their term of duty. We wash in the bore stream so loaded with salts that no soap will lather, and afterwards we gather round the steaming billies on the cook's fire, and tickle his temper by getting in his way. We eat off tin plates and drink from tin pannikins when resting our backs against rolled swags, or when squatting on our spurred boot-heels. For one short hour we may lounge and smoke and yarn.

Tim, the burly-framed boss drover, silently reviews the remaining part of the long journey; the water supplies which may be utilized and those forbidden; the camps to be made; the districts to be loitered across because they are favoured with good ground feed, and those which must be hurried across on date.

Joe, the horse-tailer, bites at his tobacco plug. Blue, the sandy-haired, fresh-complexioned reciter of bush ballads, rolls a cigarette down his trousers leg with lightning rapidity, tosses high the cylinder, to catch it expertly with his lips by one end when it falls. He never does that when Harry of the one eye is near with a stockwhip in his hand. There are Ted and Alec: the one fat yet nimbly active; the other lean and tall, slow in speech and movement, yet tigerishly agile when cutting out calves at branding time. They are a fair sample of bushmen; keen, efficient, light-hearted, and generous. All eyes are clear. Every face is superbly healthy. They talk in quiet, confident tones, and one feels honoured to be one of the company.

The nights and days are governed by set routine. Star-lit nights and black nights; hard, brilliant days, and days when the air is balmy and the sunlight is subdued by a high-level haze which foretells days of wind and dust, when the herd is difficult to distinguish against the blurred background of sandhill and scrub. Every day produces its little scenic surprises, vying with the cattle, which produce their surprises, too.

The beasts walk up and over and down the endless sand-ridges divided by the narrow flats. At long last we sight the Barrier Range to the south-east. Slowly we skirt the Range that is tinged blue by distance. We come to a wide saltbush plain extending to the sharply-cut horizon. We cross deep water-gutters and gum-lined dry creeks. Before us, growing out of the plain like mushrooms, rise the houses comprising the town of Cockburn, some three hundred miles from Adelaide. Now and then, white steam-puffs from a locomotive hang against the background of blue sky.

In a day or so all the cattle will have been trucked for the city, including that troublesome black and white steer.

Camels at Upfield's Albermarle Station, photographed by his mate E. V. Whyte 1920.

Aboriginal stockman with camels at Bundooma Siding, Northern Territory 1932.

6.

AN AUSTRALIAN CAMEL STATION

*Situated about 150miles east
of Geraldton in Western Australia*

IN Australia, sheep and cattle stations are common enough; but it rarely happens that a large area of land is used exclusively for the breeding of camels. One such place, Dromedary Hill Camel Station in Western Australia, provides a unique experience for even the blasé traveller. There these animals are stocked and broken in for use in drawing carts and buckboards. Moreover, the station has scenic beauties that await proper appreciation and exploitation by the producers of moving pictures. To be sure there are no mountain vistas, no views of sparkling lakes or misty waterfalls ; but there is to be seen in miniature the same wild country that is found along the border of Mexico and the U.S.A. Dromedary Hill is run by a Government Department controlling all the vermin fences in the State, but financial stringency resulting from the universal trade depression caused the temporary removal of the camels to a station farther north, so that, at the time of writing, on the country where camels once roamed cattle and sheep have their being.

The station is named from the animals born and reared there, not from the three-hundred-feet high, twin-humped granite mound bearing a few cork trees, scattered tussock grass and an annual vegetation that is dependent on seasonal rain to grow at all. In Australia the dromedary has played a great part in the country's exploration and development.

Having received instructions by "mulga wire" to return to the Camel Station and there assist the man then in charge to train two young camels to draw a buckboard for one of the fence inspectors, it was with keen satisfaction that I unharnessed the pair of camels from my boundary rider's covered dray and humped the gear into the comfortable, four-roomed, stone-built homestead. That was towards the end of June, when even the blacks prefer a roof and four walls—assuming they can command such a shelter—to the cold, wind-swept and often rainswept bushlands.

It was first necessary to muster all the stock, a business requiring not a little understanding of the camel's mentality. Your expert camel-man is one who never under-estimates the intelligence of the beast, and when handling it never affords it a chance "to catch him bending." When the mob of camels had been edged into the home paddock, the remainder of the mustering was done on foot and without haste, for, once the beasts suspected any design on their liberty, two vicious beasts would have led a "break back," when a hundred well-horsed stockmen could not have stopped them. The mob, eventually, was driven into the wide mouth of the runway to the stoutly built yards where the camels could be forced onward should they display any objection.

The two animals selected for training were young bull camels, partly broken in several years before when they had been included in a team of sixteen harnessed to a heavy wagon. They were quiet enough to be touched, although still fearful of man; and consequently they offered good material, although others of their kind had been spoiled when calves by the boundary riders, who worked their mothers. The spoiled ones had no fear of man, and no respect for him either.

For a week the novices were harnessed in turn with an old camel to a cumbersome dray loaded with sand, and throughout this first week all possible vices were to be discovered—biting, striking, even calculated attempts at murder. Like the elephant, the camel is a reasoning beast, quickly amenable to kindness allied with firmness, and not quickly forgetful of cruelty.

The second stage was less interesting and much more uncomfortable for the drivers. The youngsters were harnessed to a heavy buckboard and driven round and round Dromedary Hill on a track long used for this purpose. Hour after hour, walking or easily trotting, with frequent halts to teach them to stand quietly, they were thus slowly hardened, but the cold winds of July caused the drivers often to wish that the team would bolt or otherwise misbehave.

During the final stage, the now docile animals were constantly halted before a gate, driven through the gateway, and again halted beyond it while the gate was being closed. They thus learnt to stand still so that anyone in sole charge of them could trust them to stand when he had to open and close a gate.

I SHALL never forget Dromedary Hill as I knew it throughout one September. Situated in the centre of a small plain on which grows salt-bush, for several weeks it was covered completely with buttercups and, when seen from rising ground two miles distant, it appeared just like a gigantic nugget of pure gold resting on the dark-green velvet of the scrub. Climbing to either of the twin granite summits, one is definitely impressed by the magnitude of Australia, after having for long lived in the narrow aisles of the mulga forest. Beyond the rims of the plain, on which the rabbit warrens show in big, light-brown patches, the scrub extends its unbroken mantle to the clear-cut horizon. The limit of vision is but ten to twenty miles, because the hill and the small plain lie in a land depression; but beyond the horizon eastward stretch two thousand miles of bush before the farms of New South Wales are reached. Northward the bush extends for nearly a thousand miles to its meeting-place with the ocean. Westward it rolls over the break-away country for two hundred miles and more to the farms lying along the coastal strip fringing the Indian Ocean, while to the south civilization comes nearest in the scattered wheat farms one hundred and fifty miles away.

Circumstances placed me in charge of this small property— there were only about thirty thousand acres within its boundaries —and opportunity was presented to explore the break-away country cutting across its western extremities.

Once off the hill plain, the scrub grows thickly, the trees averaging in height but thirty feet. I came abruptly upon outcrops of ironstone and quartz that formed natural clearings where the sunlight was reflected by the mica particles embedded in the stone. Every clearing would then resemble a jeweller's show-window. Flannel flowers, blue-point flowers, and the white everlastings were everywhere.

One becomes quickly tired of riding in close-pressing mulga scrub, and belts of bogeta bush, and the spiky-leafed wait-a-bit trees. Absent are far horizons, rounded hills, long vistas; one cannot see the wood for the trees. The sky is but a narrow circle and is never clearly seen; on all sides is the amber wall of bush, stained with greens and browns. One is free and yet confined. The scrub is like a prison cell from which there is seemingly no escape.

And then the wall ahead begins to pale. Ahead there is light, space, and freedom. It is as a door opening, and eagerly we reach its threshold to step out upon a narrow, rock-floored ledge above a Western Australian break-away. From confinement to freedom; from shadow into blazing sunlight; the walls have fallen down, and after all there are great spaces to stir the imagination, to revivify the childish longing for power to fly into a stormy sunset.

THERE lies a strip of land eighty miles in length and ten miles in width that, when man was not, sank three hundred feet nearer the heart of the world. Down there in that magnificent valley the salt-bush shimmers like a rolling grey-green sea, on which the patches of white quartz chips are like racing sea horses. On stands above a sea that never was, a sea of salt-bush caressing a rugged coast of thrusting headlands, shrinking bays, and detached islands floating on the mirage.

Fifty to one hundred feet high rises the perpendicular face of the cliff that marks the sinking of the break-away of this section of earth. At its foot the weather and the wind have scooped caves, providing shelter for all the wild things from summer heat and winter storms. Often the caves are masked by huge blocks and slabs of rock fallen from the break-away face, and a tour of some of the caves will reveal on their sandy floors tracks of kangaroos and dingoes. From the cliff the ground slopes downward to the wide flats and the maze of dry creeks which reach to the opposing break-away, presenting a seemingly impassable barrier across the valley.

To the north, the sweep of the great bight on which one stands ends at a beetling headland ; to the south it terminates in a shelving rampart of brown rubble thrusting from it three large, scrub-capped islands. Far away along the valley, rising from a mirage sea, a weathered granite outcrop appears like some medieval castle, battlemented, turreted. Due west, a sentinel on the opposing "coast," stands a towering round hill, and farther southward a black headland thrusts outward across the valley like the head of a snake wishing to cross the strait.

What a country! To the south-east Youanmi; to the north Paynesville; north-west lies Mount Magnet, and to the west Yalgoo. All are towns created by the discovery of gold. Gold lies all about one. Why, the heart of one of those islands spurned by this "coast" might be of gold!

Arthur Upfield's camel dray, showing his writing desk, on the left, as published in *Walkabout* on March 1 1935.

An unusually large kangaroo hide.

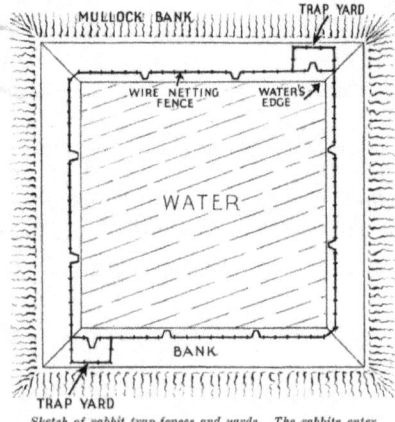

Sketch of rabbit trap-fences and yards. The rabbits enter through the "V"-shaped openings, and after drinking pass along between the water and the fence into the trap-yards.

7.

TRAPPING FOR FUR

A LITTLE-KNOWN industry in Australia, but one of extraordinary fascination to the operator, is the trapping of foxes and rabbits for the fur markets of the world. In North America trapping furred animals has secured the glamour of romance with its background of snow and ice; but here in Australia the rabbit and the fox are Public Enemies Numbers One and Two, and the industry is regarded as being beyond the pale. The fact that the skins of these animals have brought millions of pounds to Australia since the Great War is seldom mentioned.

The fur trapper earns more money than the station hand and the stockman, the artisan and the clerk, but he labours much harder and for longer hours when he is "on fur." He experiences a fever of activity similar to the gold-fever known by the prospector when "on gold." He works every minute of the day and begrudges the necessary time spent in eating and sleeping. Gold, however, which has been hidden in the ground for countless ages, will not disappear overnight or run away; but a real harvest of fur is brought about by a set of climatic conditions which might change in an hour and reduce the supply of fur to a comparative trickle.

The trapper's day begins (officially) at nine o'clock in the morning. He has eaten breakfast beside the camp-fire built a short distance from his sleeping tent and skin tent, and his motor truck or horse-drawn buckboard. The sky is cloudless; the air is clear as crystal glass; the sun is delightfully cool. Dawn has revealed white frost. It is mid-May in the far west of New South Wales.

Having rolled and lit the inevitable cigarette, the trapper slips through his belt the handle of a light tomahawk, picks up a chaff bag, and sets out for the trap-line he laid down the previous day. In this instance he is operating along the shores of a great dry lake forming a basin in high plain country. In circumference the lake is six or seven miles, and every yard of every mile of the low sandhills forming the shore is honeycombed by rabbits. The autumn rains have failed, and tens of thousands of rabbits have congregated in the vicinity of the lake on account of the herbal rubbish growing on its dry bed.

Already they have eaten bare the ground for three hundred yards out from the "shore," and shortly after every dawn the eagles begin their hunt. These magnificent birds will leave the scrub-line and fly low above the herbal rubbish when out of it stream the rabbits that have spent the night there. In their thousands, they race across the bare ground to the shore burrows, massed like sheep being driven to the yards, the eagles above them sluggishly flapping their great wings and seldom failing to pounce on their breakfast.

Arrived at the camp end of his trap-line, the trapper proceeds to pull up his traps and carry them in lots of twenty-four to the far end, where he begins to set another line. Each trap is set at a burrow opening, and each is marked by. a small stick pushed into the ground a few feet back from it. Of every hole thus guarded by a trap there are ten or twelve left free, and the hundred traps extend for some four hundred yards. When he sets his last trap, he makes a trail on the ground with a stick from trap to trap back to the first one set.

Innumerable crows have been watching him. So have many eagles, to whom one rabbit has been a poor breakfast. At intervals along the previous day's trap-line, the skinned carcasses have been gathered and hidden from the birds with tree branches, and now there is to be prepared a feast for them, for, be it understood, the beautiful wedge-tailed eagle, sometimes erroneously called a hawk, is considered Public Enemy Number Three in the sheep country, and a price of half a crown is placed on its head.

On the higher ground above the old trap-line, the trapper proceeds to lay down circle traps. A bait of several rabbit carcasses is pinned to the ground with wire stakes, and around this bait are arranged rabbit traps, the business ends within a foot of the bait and the iron spikes at the ends of the trap chains driven into the ground. When the circle trap is laid, there is nothing to be seen other than the bait, and, when the trapper has gone, an eagle will alight on the ground near the bait and walk to it. If it does not walk directly to a trap, it will do so when it begins to tug and struggle with the bait.

It is saddening to see these great birds thus destroyed, but any trapper's heart has long been hardened by their terrible attacks on newly-born, defenceless lambs.

It is noon when the trapper has prepared his daily trap-line, and in camp once more he eats a hasty meal of cold meat and baking-powder bread. Because it is early winter, he may indulge in the luxury of butter, but fresh milk and vegetables are unknown. If vegetables were procurable it is very doubtful if he would spend time preparing and cooking them.

The meal having been bolted like his breakfast, the trapper gives himself no rest. How can he? The sun rushes across the sky from its rising to its setting. There is never any catching up with Time, although the effort to do so is ceaseless. Fox baits to be laid that night have to be made with "marbles" of sheep's caul-fat dipped in powdered strychnine; rabbit skins and fox pelts have to be removed from the drying ground and packed away in the skin tent; and the skins procured have to be slipped over U-shaped pieces of wire, the points of which are thrust into the ground, to dry, and the pelts tacked fur-downwards on a hard clay-pan that they may dry and retain proper marketable shape afterwards.

Already it is three o'clock, and the trap-line cries for attention. Before it is reached, sluggishly-rising eagles flap upward from the vicinity of the circle traps. One trap has imprisoned an eagle by either foot and the tip of one wing. Another holds three birds. Yet another has caught a wretched crow, for which no bonus is offered. Ten shillings already for the trouble of setting five or six circle traps!

Reaching the end of the trap-line, the trapper is guided by the sticks to each of his traps, and out of the hundred set he takes forty rabbits. Before the depression, the price of rabbit skins averaged a shilling a dozen. He takes the rabbits to the line of box trees bordering the lake, and there he skins them, making two major cuts and two small snips before flicking off the skin. About four seconds elapse between taking up the rabbit and dropping its rolled skin into the chaff-bag.

Back again to the camp. It will have to be moved in a day or so after the trap-line, and this will cause an annoying waste of time, but time less wasted than if he had to walk more than a mile to the trap-line.

The skins are bowed on the wire U's, and another hour is given to those needing transference from the drying-ground to the skin tent. The sun is falling out of the sky down to the timbered horizon. The trapper's legs are crying out for rest, but the fur fever drives him on and on. Each little rabbit skin is a grain of gold, each fox pelt is a small nugget. The eagles are nothing much; they pay the tucker and petrol bills. The tally-book says that yesterday he trapped a hundred and five rabbits and seven foxes: the day before ninety-nine rabbits and nine foxes: the day before that a hundred and thirteen rabbits and seven foxes. One hundred and twenty-one rabbits is the record this season, but that night he obtained only one fox. Forty rabbits! He has got forty today so far. He might well pass the record. On and on and on! On and beat the sun! A man might just as well sell his bed and buy another pair of boots. What is the use of a bed, anyway?

Should there be one small cloud in the sky, the trapper will frown and pray that it is not the forerunner of rain clouds. Rain would compel the majority of the rabbits to scatter far and wide across the plain to dig out old burrows and begin to breed. The foxes would scatter after them; and, within a few weeks, trapping would be stopped by the young rabbits springing the traps. But these days of May and June are diamond days, and the nights are calm and brittle with frost.

It is now five o'clock. In another hour the sun will set. In all the twenty-four hours there is now half an hour the trapper may call his own. He boils the billy for tea and snatches a meal, and for the first time since starting the day takes pleasure in smoking a cigarette.

Half-past five! The trapper banks the fire before leaving camp with the tin of fox baits and a sheep's head attached to the end of a light rope. In his circle traps are two more eagles.

Along the trap-line thirty-five rabbits await their doom. Having reset the circle traps, and removed and reset those traps that have caught rabbits, he finds it is almost six o'clock by the time he reaches the far end of the trap-line.

The gathered skins in the bag he leaves there to be picked up later. The sun sets in an orange bed, leaving the glowing sky vacant. At once twilight begins to deepen, and immediately it is dark the foxes will leave their holes out on the plain and come padding to the lake to catch rabbits. Before they come, the fox trail has to be laid, and yet if it is put down too early the watching crows will steal the baits.

Well above the line of burrows, the trapper hesitates. It is not quite dark enough to frustrate the crows. The lake still gleams with greens and greys, and the high plain still retains the sheen of the orange sheet of sky. Only beneath the box trees between lake and plain is it dark.

Now! The trapper begins to drag the sheep's head—or it might be a liver—towards the camp, keeping parallel with the trap-line. At every hundred paces he leaves two of the poison-baits and marks the spot on the ground with a boot-heel. The baits lie on the trail, which is distinct enough for human eyes to follow, and foxes' noses to follow, too.

Why two baits? Why not one, or more than two?

A fur-getter has to be something of a naturalist should he wish to make a living. He has to study the habits of the furred animal he desires to trap. Should he leave single baits at intervals, a fox in running the trail might snatch one up without pause and carry it daintily between its teeth until the bitter taste of the poison would cause it to drop the bait. When there are two baits, it must swallow the first to pick up the second; whilst, if several baits are put down at one place, the overdose of strychnine would defeat the object for which it was put down. The fox would get rid of the baits and run for miles, and perhaps for many hours, before dropping. As the trapper began the fox trail at the far end of the trap-line, he finishes it near the camp.

It is now quite dark. The foxes are out! "Whorl—whorl!" "Whorl—whorl!" The cry is slightly imitative of the bark of a dog. "Quok—quok—quok!" Now it is not unlike the cry of a duck. When two foxes meet and fight over a rabbit one has caught, they utter "Quex—quex!" "Quex—quex!" ' In his lonely camp, warming himself while the billy comes to the boil once more, the trapper's eyes narrow when he believes by the night-sounds that more than one fox is running his trail.

Beyond the boundaries of the firelight, which here reveals the twisted trunk of a box tree and there the white tents and the truck, the night is as black as the ace of spades. The trap-line is too distant to hear the squeals of rabbits, but he knows that thousands of rabbits have left the burrows to feed on the lake, and that dozens of foxes are there, too, stalking the rabbits.

Another meal! An hour is then occupied in baking a loaf of bread and boiling or baking meat for the morrow.

At seven o'clock the trapper sets off again, this time lighted on his way by a hurricane lamp. The surroundings are vastly different from those of daylight. The fog has distorted the trees and hidden the sky-line. Now is apparent the wisdom of erecting little sticks behind the traps and making on the ground a connecting mark. Having reached a noted tree where the connecting trail ends, the trapper finds that in the lamplight this trail stands out vividly. By following it, he makes his way from trap to trap, and loses no time in looking for the marking-sticks.

When he arrives at the far end, he picks up the bag containing the skins, and with it and the twenty-two rabbits this visit has added to the tally, he withdraws a little and lights a fire, for he must allow two hours to pass before making the final inspection for the night—and it is not worth while returning to camp.

Now and then a rabbit squeals, and the peculiar sound informs the lounging man that his traps are working. Out on the lake a rabbit screams shrilly, and the timbre of it is different. Out there in the black nothingness of night, a fox has caught a rabbit and killed. An imaginative man can picture the drama of the wild. He must hold himself in iron control above his lonely fire, before which he is struggling to keep awake, when there bursts a rising horrible shriek of pain that rushes outward across the lake and the plain behind with nerve-shattering volume. An Australian curlew has passed.

At half-past ten, the trapper rouses. It will not do—he has almost fallen asleep. With the lamp to aid him, he returns over the trap-line and gathers a further ten skins to add to the day's total. It is well after eleven when camp is reached, and then .the billy must be warmed and coal-black tea, sweetened with sugar, sipped as a nightcap. The alarm clock will go off at five.

Five hours' sleep is the rule. This limit has been permitted for several weeks, and the trapper is semi-dazed for want of sleep. But he must beat the crows in the morning. At any hour the rain may come, and then he can sleep for a week or a fortnight. Before day breaks, the trapper has eaten his breakfast.

Over the lake hangs a low mist. A wide-awake crow—the ever present arch-enemy of every trapper—caws to its mates to be up and doing, and to see what the human was dropping on the fox-trail late the evening before. With half a dozen chaff-bags on his shoulder, and with the empty bait-tin under an arm, the trapper sets off for the camp end of the fox-trail when dawn is painting the sky, whilst yet the earth sleeps in darkness. The crows will not wait for daylight, and it has now become a daily race between them and him. If the crows take the baits that may be left by the foxes, precious time will be wasted looking for the foxes that presumably took them. If the crows, and after them the eagles, reach the carcass of a fox before the trapper, the pelt will be ruined in less than fifteen seconds.

It is half-light when he reaches the fox trail, barely light enough for him to follow it. His gaze is divided by the trail and the bare ground on either side, and so he comes to the first mark made by his boot-heel to indicate where he has placed the last of the twin fat balls. They are gone! Good! There must be a fox lying somewhere near. He scrapes a mark to denote that here the baits have been taken. A crow flies overhead, cawing mockingly. On again to the next baits.. They, too, are gone. Ah—there lies a fox! The trapper runs to it to lay over the beautiful fur one of the chaff bags in order to defeat the crows. Back then to the trail and onward to the next mark! Over there another fox! Here both baits left! And so he- runs or trots to retrieve all the untaken baits and cover the precious fur with the chaff-bags. He has this morning obtained eleven gold nuggets—red-brown and silver-brown furs destined to cling to milady's neck. Fur! No woman thrills to the touch of fur as does the trapper. Here is a beauty, its dark-brown points tipped with silver! If they dye this black, they should be shot! See how the light sparkles all red and auburn on the soft coat! The trapper slips his fingers through the fur and for a moment has forgotten the little gold-nugget it represents. Carefully, yet rapidly, he removes the pelts; carefully he rolls them into balls of fur and deposits them in a bag. On the carcasses there has not been left a particle of fur, on the pelts there has not been made one careless knife-cut.

Now he works back to the camp over the trap-line, here and there taking out a rabbit, springing all the traps with the sole of a boot. A circle-trap has caught a fox, and it has to be killed and skinned. By eight o'clock the trapper is eating breakfast: by nine he has wire-bowed the rabbit-skins and tacked the fox-pelts to a hard claypan with wire nails. When dry, they will come up as stiff as cardboard and as perfect in shape as the tiger-skin on the floor of a big-game-hunter's study. Once again the sun is sliding up the wall of the sky. It never stops: only when a man is engaged in distasteful work does the sun stop still. Already it is nine o'clock, and the new day begins with the moving forward of all the traps.

THE scene changes, the months slip by. It is February, and the Inland lies scorched by a heat-wave. The water in the gilgie holes and the shallow creeks has long since dried up, and all the birds and the animals must drink at man-made reservoirs.

At the foot of a gentle ground-slope, fifteen thousand cubic yards of earth have been scooped up into high bank^ enclosing a great hole in the ground. In shape the hole is, perfectly square. The mullock banks forming the four sides are symmetrically fashioned. Through one side a large iron pipe admits water from the drain channels directed to it—when it rains. At this time a mere foot of muddy water lies in the bottom of the tank or dam.

All day long two trappers have laboured in the airless bottom of the tank. Despite the terrific heat, they have erected a flimsy netted fence enclosing the sheet of water. Here and there the fence has been built to form a wide V, the point of each V coming to within six inches of the water. At the point of each V a small hole has been cut in the wire mesh. At opposite corners an outward leading V leads into a large stoutly-built trap-yard six feet in height and eight feet square. By sundown the stage has been set for the most amazing drama Australia has to offer, certain climatic conditions and the life-curves of certain animal cycles being necessary to stage it.

For three years the rabbits have been multiplying, from the original scattered pairs to countless thousands. The lack of rain over eight or nine months has compelled them to mass in the vicinity of dams and water-holes in creeks. With the rabbits' growth in numbers so have grown numerically the foxes and the eagles, and in this blistering February all animal life is concentrated at widely-separated points.

Standing on top of the mullock bank, when the sheet of water in the tank lies sixty feet below, the observer sees that all around the tank the country has been eaten bare by the stock and the massed animals. The stock has been removed, because at any hour the foot of muddy water will disappear. When that occurs, the kangaroos and foxes will migrate to another tank, but the rabbit host will perish. The trappers are again fighting the sun, not for its seeming speed across the heavens, but on account of its power of evaporation of water and its consequent power to kill.

THE stage being set, the trappers' day begins. From experience, they can estimate that, should the water last one week, at this tank they will catch from sixteen to twenty thousand rabbits. When the sun is setting, when the sky is one great blaze of apricot, the men arrive with their canvas water-bags, skin bags, skinning knives, and shotguns. They take positions at opposite corners of the tank, at the foot of the mullock bank on the narrow strip of level ground above the tank. Their task is to prevent the thirsty kangaroos from smashing down the flimsy fence and permitting the rabbits to escape.

Comes now the coloured twilight. It stains the sheet of water with bars of yellow and silver. The mullock-banks on their western sides are painted crimson and amber and grey. At the edge of the water grey-backed, scarlet-breasted galah parrots drink with clockwork action. It has often been stated that they drink on the wing: they do not. They take no notice of the men—no living thing, bar the kangaroos, will take notice of the men this night. Colour! It is as colourful as a scene from a modern musical play. And then, in a second as it were, the colours vanish, leaving the dull-grey tint of land, the dull silver of water, and the soft steel-blue of sky.

Over the summit of the mullock-bank now slips a swift-moving shadow. It is the first of a great army of advancing rabbits, which this night must drink or else perish before another sunset. Without once pausing, the shadow glides straight down to the fence. Another shadow slips over the bank and down to the fence, and another, and yet others. The trappers lie on their backs and smoke. One catches a rabbit with his hand when it is about to pass him. The rodent squeals and struggles, and, when released, it continues its journey to the water as though the incident had not hap-pened. It has acted like a soldier, disciplined by thirst.

Now the stars are out. The details of the tank are merged into a dark blur, down which ceaselessly slide drops of ink. It it not possible to see, but we know what is going on down at the fence. The rabbits are running along the outside of it. Some are stretching upward against it as though measuring its height. Here they are gathered into small masses of fur. Then one reaches a V, to enter and run to its point, where beyond the small hole lies within six inches *the water it must drink.* For the first time it hesitates. Then it wriggles its fore-quarters through the hole and begins to lap like a cat.

Another rabbit, on entering the V and hearing the other drinking, runs to it and bites its rump. The first thereupon wriggles right through and, to avoid wetting its feet, must turn to one side where there is a yard of space between the water and the fence. Others follow. Through all the V's they are passing like sand-grains in an egg-glass. When they have taken their fill, they turn to go back and meet the fence. There is no way over or under it. The position of the opening in the V's is too close to the water, and is also too far back in the opposite direction, to allow them to pause at these small openings. But presently, on running along the fence in frantic effort to escape, they reach an outward-placed V, through which they pass into either one of the stout trap-yards.

The trappers are now alert. It is pitch dark, but the summit of the mullock-bank presents a faint outline against the starry sky, a sky-line on which presently grows a monstrous thing between a giant spider and crab, a thing from Mars, a horrible, silent thing. Beside it moves another, and several yards from it yet another. And then one of the fearsome shapes resolves, changes into a silhouette of great beauty—a kangaroo sitting bolt upright, watching, suspicious. The men are so placed that each commands two sides of the encompassing mullock bank, and, unless stupidly careless, they cannot shoot each other. Accustomed to shoot without gun-sights, they keep the kangaroos from reaching the fence.

Out from the bottom of the tank comes a ceaseless murmur, caused by the padding of thousands of frantic rabbits. When the murmur rises to a low roar, an unseen fox announces his arrival by dashing among the rodents. It is disciplined by thirst, too. It takes no notice of the unlimited food. All through the terrible day, it has panted for the water. Having leapt the fence, it drinks like a dog, and as loudly. Rabbits fight for right of way, the combatants squealing. Guggle, guggle, guggle! One has inadvertently jumped into the water, and is swimming in circles, and slowly drowning.

TOWARDS midnight it is thought that there is a sufficient number in the trap-yards, say two thousand. One trapper calls to the other, and both light their hurricane lamps. By this light are seen the rodents, dotting the mullock-banks and the tank-sides. Down by the fence they are massed a yard deep. They cram into the V's. Along the inside of the fence they are pressed into smaller masses, filled with water and satisfied to lie quiet. Hundreds are drinking side by side as the galahs drank at sundown. Hundreds are running to and fro, searching for a way of escape.

Each of the eight-feet-square yards holds a solid block of rabbits three feet deep, four feet deep at the corners. The number will be enough for this night. No more can enter through the trap-yard V's, anyhow, until they are emptied.

The men raise the netted fence and string it along the tops of the supporting stakes. Thousands of rabbits are now able to escape, and thousands more are able to drink. They will all be back the next night, and to trap more than can be skinned would be a waste of good fur and better bank-notes.

Each trapper takes a yard. They climb among the rabbits. Every rabbit is picked up by one hand gripping the loins, and it is instantly killed when its neck is broken. Then, seated on the ground beside a great heap of dead rodents, each man proceeds to skin them at the average rate of two hundred an hour. When day breaks, they are found slipping the skins over the U-shaped pieces of stiff wire. Breakfast is ahead of them, and then, after they have trucked the heaps of carcasses to a far distance, they will lie down and try to sleep despite the heat and the flies.

And, away in the shade of the bordering scrub, lie panting thousands of animals, tortured by thirst, waiting, waiting for the merciless sun to set and vanish.

Arthur Upfield, angling off Bermagui, 1938.

8.

ANGLING FOR SWORDFISH

DEEP in the clear blue water astern of the launch, much like opal fire beneath the surface of the gem, there appeared a long and narrow blue-brown shadow, specked with points of light. For a second or two the sea-jewel kept pace with the boat; then it flashed aside and vanished. So came and passed my first glimpse of a swordfish in the wonderful fishing waters near Bermagui, New South Wales.

When in 1935, Mr. Roy Michaelis and Mr. W. G. Wallis created a world's record by landing between them nine marlin in one day—a record that has not yet been broken—Bermagui was "made." It became the centre of Australia's big-game fishing, to which have been attracted outstanding anglers like Mr. Zane Grey and Dr. Sutton, of America. Situated some 250 miles south of Sydney, Bermagui is get-at-able only by car. But what a place! What a diamond of a place! What a Mecca for all sea-fishermen!

My launch, a 37-foot, 25 h.p. craft, was afloat on twenty feet of crystal-clear water. I liked the look of her, with the two swivel chairs for fisher-men, right astern. She had that lifeboat appearance, that unsinkable look. And I liked the look of Taylor, the boatman, too; quiet, deliberate, and knowledgeable. It would take a hefty sea to capsize the craft, and a bad blow to excite its owner. Morning had broken brilliantly clear, a moderate south-easterly promising to keep down the temperature. We passed over the river-bar at eight o'clock and at once let out astern jag-lines—feathered hooks—with which to troll for bait-fish.

Several launches were out ahead of us, all trolling for bait-fish. We caught nothing while on the inner bay; but, having rounded the main headland, and riding the full ocean swells, both Taylor and I hooked a fish at the same instant. Taylor landed his—a fine two-pound sea-salmon, We had passed over the surface shoal before we could again get the hooks overboard, and the second hand swung the boat round to bring us over the shoal once more. Again both hooked a fish at the same instant, and two minutes later, we both hooked a bonito at the same time. Salmon, bonito, kingfish—all are found in shoals about this rocky headland, and jag-lines have only to be passed through them to reap a quick and rich harvest.

Already the heavy rod, with its giant steel reel containing 900 yards of cordline, was rigged and in position, and one of the bonito, weighing about a pound, was skewered to the immense hook attached to twenty feet of wire trace, which in turn was fastened to the end of the cordline. The bait was passed over the stern of the launch, now throttled down to four knots, and allowed to troll some twenty to thirty feet distant. At first the bait-fish behaved erratically, plunging beneath the surface and then jumping above it; but, after some trouble, Taylor made it skim the surface, like a hydroplane. From the extremity of poles thrust outward to port and starboard, light ropes trolled brightly-coloured cylinders of wood called teasers. Thus, to a fish deep in the remarkably clear water, the two teasers and the bait-fish would appear to be a small shoal playfully following the launch.

The angler's business is to sit in his bucket-seat and astride the rod, with body-harness to hand and ready, to be pulled on and attached to the reel, and gloves ready for his hands, which are likely to be burned by a racing line if not protected. Thereafter it is up to him to watch his bait-fish and that quarter of the sea astern of the boat, leaving the two launchmen to keep a look-out ahead and abeam for a fin.

Thus is set the stage for a fight with a swordfish or shark, a fight between a frail man armed with a cane-rod and a cord-line—no stronger than one I have broken when attempting to land a twenty-pound schnapper—and a fish weighing anything from a hundred and fifty to four hundred pounds or more. [Australia's record swordfish weighed 672 pounds.— Ed.] It will be a fight in which the odds are very much in favour of the fish, most especially the swordfish, which is far more difficult to bring to the gaff than any shark.

Tensed by the excitement of anticipation, I sat and watched the trolled bait-fish and the heaving sea astern. Hour followed hour, and no great fish took interest in the bait-fish or in the dancing teasers. We trolled this day some sixty miles and off-shore for ten miles, but never a fin did we see. Taylor and his mate were not less disappointed than I was.

The next day the wind was less strong, coming from the north, and we trolled up to Montague Island, which is about sixteen miles north of Bermagui, and about five miles off the coast. The striking peculiarities about this coast are its ruggedness and the clarity of the water washing it. The edge of the Continental Shelf here runs close to land, and beyond the shelf; the depth is tremendous. Hence there is no green water a mile or so offshore. Blue, vivid blue, is the sea beneath the sun; beneath the clouds it is silver-grey—

THE comparative, shallows, about Montague Island provide- spawning grounds for the small fish. So to them come the huge shoals of tuna and schnapper and sea-salmon. After these come the sharks: the tiger, the grey nurse, the thresher, the mako, and the hammerhead. About Christmas-time there appear the several species of swordfish, to remain till the end of March. They come down from the north-east ocean fastnesses when the water becomes warm, and they return to the north-east. When a swordfish is hooked, it invariably dashes away to the north-east and to no other point of the compass.

"Hi! Look at that!" shouts Taylor's mate. He indicates, half a mile distant, a patch of water seemingly torn by a wind-squall, but actually disturbed by a shoal of racing fish.

"There's a big fellow after them," Taylor shouts from the wheel-house. "Look how they're going!"

Then the chaser appears—a dark, slim form that shoots above the surface and plunges upon the shoal. Up it comes. again, again to plunge in white foam—a swordfish striking downward with its sword at the madly-racing small-fry, smashing them, then to speed back and devour the slain at leisure.

The engine kicks the launch, at fast speed toward the spot where the giant fish was last seen. The mate clings to the swaying mast; Taylor at the wheel stands tense. The novice is requested bluntly to watch the trolling bait-fish and the sea astern, and to shout at the appearance of a fin. For half an hour the launch is steered in wide curves and shorter circles, like a destroyer hunting a submarine, but, we do not again see the swordfish.

Seven or eight miles out at sea two launches were trolling in the deep water. Another was trolling south of us, and two others were at work far to the north. Their mastheads were bare of the bunting that announces a catch.

Round about two o'clock Taylor directed attention to an enormous shoal of fish.

"Tunny," he said, giving the local pronunciation of tuna.

A great arc of the sea to the south-east of us was lashed black and white as though by a fierce wind.

"Going to give 'em a go?" asked the mate; and Taylor looked at me, as I was hiring for big-game fishing. At my nod he sent the launch at speed towards the shoal, called the mate to take the wheel, then came aft to make ready the jag-lines. The bait-fish was drawn in and the feathered hooks let out astern.

LOOKING forward, I was presently able to see these famous tuna, and I recalled with a thrill that Mr. Zane Grey had caught with rod and line in these very waters a yellow-fin tuna weighing 91 lb. In extent the shoal must have been fully a mile in length and half-a-mile in width. The fish could be seen darting about just below the surface, yellow-smeared streaks of white, bars of blue and of green. Here the fish moved in line abreast like soldiers; there they milled like a mob. Invisible knives cut the tops of the swells, and down in the troughs the water was whitened and blackened in agitation.

The speed of the launch was reduced, and then astern could be seen part of the shoal. There is no mistaking the bite of a tunny. Both lines hooked a fish at the same instant. The cord-line cut and burned my hands. At first it was impossible to haul in; I could but hold on to these great fighting fish and wish I wielded a trout-rod and line instead of a hand-line. Then far down in the deep could be seen the hooked fish being drawn upward, the countless others coming on behind it, up and up to the very surface of the sea, from which was taken as beautiful a fish as might be imagined, weighing in the vicinity of twelve pounds.

We could have caught tunny until we were exhausted or had sunk the launch with weight of fish. In that one shoal must have been sufficient fish to feed all Australia for a week.

As the sun was westering, we made southward to Bermagui. The other boats and other anglers were all making for port, their mastheads still naked of bunting—a blue flag to, announce the capture of a swordfish, a red one for the capture of a shark. Slowly Montague Island sank into the gold-laced sea; slowly, very slowly, the cloud-capped Dromedary Mountain slipped northward along Horseshoe Bay.

Beyond the breakers next morning the bay water appeared to be as calm as any lake. "The glass is falling quickly. We'll get a southerly buster before evening," Taylor called in greeting as he supervised the loading of petrol.

A southerly buster! There was no smallest sign to the new-chum of its coming, but the barometer in the engine-house never lies, and Taylor never treats it flippantly. Outside, the river was like glass, while beyond the bar across its mouth, the sea was a cloth of diamonds.

We were soon trolling for bait-fish in company with other launches. Supplied with bait-fish, we put out the coloured teasers, and over the stern dropped the great baited hook to skim the water astern.

Taylor was doubtful whether to troll northward about Montague Island or south and then seaward of the Brothers Rocks. A very light wind was coming down from the north-east, barely touching the summits of the long swell; but along the southern horizon lay a bank of soft, white cloud, which appeared to be quite innocent of evil to the innocent at sea. A wise seaman never takes avoidable risks; a wise launchman always avoids if possible giving his patron unnecessarily unpleasant fishing conditions. As big-game fish are to be encountered anywhere off this coast at this time of the year, Taylor likes to troll towards a coming wind, so that, if forced back to port by bad weather, his boat has not to be driven into mountainous seas.

We decided to go north.

During the forenoon we trolled in vain.

Immediately after lunch, out went the coloured teasers, and the bait-fish was sent to troll astern like a small speed-boat. We were less than a mile from Montague Island when a great fish appeared.

"A shark! Here he comes!" I shouted.

"It's a swordie, not a shark," Taylor cried joyously. "Remember what I told you, now."

A dozen yards behind the skimming bail-fish had appeared a dorsal fin, slate-grey in colour, stream-lined like a knife. The bait-fish seemed to make a spurt, as though alive and sensing its clanger. My scalp tingled, and my mind flogged itself to remember all the advice I had been given. I was sickened by the thought! That I might make a foolish mistake at the crucial moment. With incredible speed the fin cut across the water towards the bait-fish. It came alongside the bait without deflecting it. I was conscious that the teasers had disappeared, had been pulled aboard by Taylor or his assistant. The fin dropped back from the bait-fish, and I wanted to yell my disappointment. Blindly I clipped the harness to the steel reel and then slipped on the gloves. Farther back dropped the fin-a yard, two, three yards. And then on it came once more, like a greyhound after a hare. There was something dread fully inevitable about it. Swiftly it drew to one side and a little behind the bait-fish, and then over the bait-fish I lifted a blue-brown spear. For a second it hovered thus, and then the sword smashed into the water beside the bait-fish as the whitish throat of the "swordie" turned outward and the gummy jaws closed about the bait. There was a flurry of water, and then the line raced away out of the reel with a long, high-pitched scream.

At once the launch-engine was slipped into neutral. Abruptly the scream of the reel stopped. I began to count. One, two, three, four, five - the swordie had turned the bait-fish in its jaws, down there in the deep, in order to swallow it head first. Six, seven, eight, nine - now it was chewing the bait-fish like a human before swallowing. Soon I must strike. However I resisted the temptation of striking when the swordfish had first taken the bait, I do not know. I account myself a man of iron on that score. To have done so would merely have dragged bait and hook clear of the gummy mouth pressed about if. Ten, eleven, twelve — the line went slack. The fish had felt the hook - or the wire-trace in the act of masticating, and, abruptly suspicious, was about to come up at express speed, to leap above water, in the attempt to throw out this strange food.

NOW was the moment. Madly I reeled in the slack of the line. Then, with a wide backward sweep of the rod-tip, I struck, and felt, the tug of the fish's weight on the line. For a period of one second the reel screamed despite all I could do to brake it. Again the line ran out beyond me, went slack. Then, out of the ocean sprang the fish to hover for what appeared an age in mid-air before falling back with a mighty splash.

"You've got him!" shouted the exultant second hand.

"Fight him!" urged Taylor. "Feel him! Feel him!"

Feel him! I could *feel* him all right. Inexperienced as I was, I was in agony when watching the bend of the rod, which I had been able to bend myself only by exerting all my power on it. I was in an agony, too, about the taut line. Did I have the reel-brake on too hard? Would it snap the line at some weak point and lose me my fish? Out went the line, two, three, four hundred yards, much more line than I should have allowed to escape front the reel, before the marlin stopped. Now began my proper job. Bringing the tip of the rod as high over my head as I could raise it, I let it fall almost to the sea and at the same time reeled hard on the temporary slack thus gained. And so it went on—up with the rod-tip, then down again, and reel in hard. Thus I gained about a hundred yards of line. Then the fish objected, and made off for fifty yards. Back I brought him for seventy-odd yards, and then again he was off for fifty yards. It was tough going, but presently I became more confident and dexterous with the rod and line, permitting my fish to get back only a yard of line for every two I gained on it.

"He's tiring," Taylor said with intense satisfaction. "So he should be; he's been on for forty minutes."

Forty minutes! Surely for thirty-five minutes time had stopped! It could have been only five minutes back that I had counted to twelve before striking.

I could still *feel* him. The fish was fast becoming tired; it came easier to my persuasion. It could have been only a little more tired than I was; but

I was exultant, already ready to drop to the floor-boards of the launch, for I knew that, barring atrocious ill-luck, I should win this battle. Half of the 900 yards of Australian-made cord had been tested most severely and found to be faultless. One flaw in that first 450 yards would have cost me my fish and broken my heart.

AGAINST the reel-brake I now was losing no line. The *feel* of the giant fish had become altered from ferocious strength to lethargic weight. Up from the surfing water came the shining brass swivel joining the cord-line to the twenty yards of wire trace. Ah! So the fish was only twenty yards below surface.

"There he is!" shouted the launchmen.

They were standing ready to take their legitimate part—one with the gaff, the other with a rope ready to noose the catch. I was, of course, still glued to the bucket-seat, and, being lower than they saw nothing until the water boiled and the fish made its last throw of the dice. I simply had to let it take a dozen yards of the line in my anxiety lest the cord might break beneath the terrific strain. And that was the finish. I was able to draw in the fish to the side of the boat and reel hard while so doing.

Five minutes later, my black marlin swordfish lay lashed across the stern of the launch, and I was gazing at the masthead from which fluttered the blue flag of conquest—the first blue flag to be flown from the masthead of a Bermagui launch for ten days.

Taylor and his mate were bubbling with satisfaction. My arms felt like lead, and pain was shooting between my shoulders and down my back. I was mentally dazed, not by fatigue but by astonishment that I had been fighting that monster of the sea for fifty-five minutes and that I actually had brought it to the gaff. And all that without possessing any previous experience of fishing save that of trout-fishing with rod and line, and shark-fishing with a half-inch rope.

The long bank of fleecy clouds seen lying along the horizon at eight o'clock was now mounting to the zenith. The clouds forming the bank were behaving strangely, rolling in and over each other. A long bar of cloud was being attracted by the summit of Dromedary Mountain as though the mountain were a magnet.

AND so, with the teasers inboard and the big hook unbaited, the launch was sent at a cruising speed of about eight knots southward to Bermagui.

We were within two miles of the home headland when the wind was seen darkening the sea to the south, just as those great shoals of fish darken the water. The edge of the dark water came racing to meet us, and, within five minutes after the first squall, the launch was nosing into a fast-rising sea. Sea-rain hailed down upon us, but what mattered short discomfort when that beautiful fish lay across the stern?

With the blue flag whipping at the masthead, we reached the jetty. Willing hands hauled the fish up to the hoist, where the secretary noted the weight and announced it as being 223 lb.—quite a nice weight for a black marlin—and gave its length as 10-ft. 1-in., and its girth as 3-ft. 9-in.

The southerly buster opened the following day with heavy seas and a strong southerly wind; but, towards noon, wind and sea went down quite a lot and fishing was begun in earnest. Taylor steered due east off-land for some twelve miles. No big fish rose to the bait; but we were passed closely by a school of more than a hundred dolphins, which must have been on feed, for they took not the smallest notice of us. There are periods when for hours no fin is sighted and the angler grows bored with the eternal watching of his trolling bait-fish and the sun-lit sea astern.

I GOT my chance with a hammerhead the following afternoon. I cannot say I was not warned what I was in for, for Taylor had often said that, for sheer brainless stubbornness, the hammerhead shark is unbeatable, and really should not be classed with game-fish as are the tiger and mako sharks. Still, they are so classed, and I wanted to land just one, and this one was allowed to come after the bait-fish, roll to one side, take it, and run.

Allowing him to pay out a hundred and fifty yards of line, I struck. It was like hitting at a bag of pollard. Then it became as though I was fastened to a tractor. When the shark wanted to go, nothing I could do would stop him. I think that a strong man, weighing about eighteen stone and using a bessemer girder for rod and wire for line, would be best suited to this-type of fishing—a man able to pull up a ton with one hand.

When I gained a foot of line, the shark took out two feet. If only it had come to the surface and fought like a gentleman, or even charged the boat and tried to eat it as the mako sometimes will do, the battle would have been more interesting. As it was, and as Taylor promised it would be, the affair was one of sheer hard labour, of heaving against a submerged mountain and reeling in by inches, and being unable to prevent loss of line without breaking it or the .expensive rod.

At the end of an hour, I got the fish in as far as the swivel, attaching the wire- trace to the cord-line—twenty feet. We saw its dorsal fin and the grey shadow of its broad back. By now I was very tired, but thankful that the job of work was all but finished. And then away swam that brute of a shark and took out more than two hundred yards of line. All over again I was forced to haul it in foot by hard-won foot, like a man walking on deep sand when he slips back half a stride for every stride gained.

And, when finally it was brought alongside, it was near death from fatigue, while I felt almost as bad. Up fluttered the red flag, and home we went without further trolling that day. I could not have fought a swordfish had one taken the bait-fish and subsequently weighed only half a hundred pounds.

An ugly brute was this shark, which was officially weighed at 380-lb., its length being 11ft., and its girth 4ft. 4in. Dr. Sutton, of America, was in before us with a hammerhead weighing 420-lb., so after all mine was but a pup. The hammerhead is well worthy of its name its eyes being situated at the extremity of its extraordinary "flipper-like" head, and its brain-mass being no larger than that of a kitten. But its mouth, smaller than that of a tiger shark, is lined with fearful teeth, which, when once fastened upon flesh, can never release it save to swallow it.

If and when another hammerhead comes after my bait-fish, I shall hastily draw inboard my trace and hook—as I did the following afternoon. One hammerhead in one's fishing experience is all-sufficient.

And so home to Bermagui for the last, time this season, assisted to port by breaking waves, which raced after us to tower high about our stern before lifting us high and thrusting us forward as though impatient of our tardiness.

One wishes Taylor and his mate *au-revoir*, not good-bye, leaving them in their snug boat, and the sharks and swordfish still masters of the vasty deep.

9.

THIS JEALOUS LAND

AUSTRALIA has never been spontaneously kind to man. It has had to be whipped and subdued by a virile white race to compel its astonishing bounty in those areas possessing the most favourable climate, and over at least two-thirds of its mass it still rules unconquered and defiant, crafty and dangerous to the unwary.

The aborigines held a strong belief in an evil spirit who pranced in the sandy columns of the whirlwinds, lurked within the mirage, and rode the clouds that race towards the sun but do not pass across its scorching face. He wore shoes of feathers glued to his feet with human blood, so that he never left any tracks when he stalked a man who had broken one of the taboos set up by the Great Ancestors in the Alchuringa Era. He was a most powerful spirit and, like the ants and the lizards, he was most active throughout the summer.

It is not strange that many white men who have lived close to the beating heart of Australia also have felt the pressure of a watchful spirit, for they have been exposed to the same conditions as were the aborigines.

The interior of Australia is not unlike a Jekyll-Hyde combination. From April to September it is a smiling, kindly Doctor Jekyll, but during October it takes the draught which for six months turns it into a Mr Hyde, armed with the Sword of the Sun.

Wise men never give Mr Hyde a chance to use his weapon upon them, but there are men who are apt to regard contemptuously anything with which they are familiar, and these provide the easy victims. Then misfortune often offers a victim in a stockman thrown from his horse and injured when the shade temperature is in the vicinity of 110° and higher.

Men have perished when their car or truck has broken down because of a dry radiator, perished because they did not take water in a bag or a tin. No one can play tiddlywinks with Mr Hyde.

When the shade temperature on a comparatively cool homestead verandah is something like 115°, anyone working in the sun is liable to feel discomfort. In that heat, rabbits forced into the sunlight are liable to be struck dead, and birds are likely to drop dead from trees. I once saw a crow fold up in flight and drop like a stone. The windless days are the worst ... which reminds me.

WHEN working on a station west of the Darling, I was ordered by the boss to take a horse-drawn dray to an old fence from which he wanted the wire. It was mid-morning on a fine day in February when I took the horse from the dray and neck-roped him to a tree. Shortly before noon I felt giddy but did not know why. After I had boiled the billy and smoked a cigarette I felt better and was fit again for work.

The work was not strenuous. I had merely to cut the wire at the strainer posts and coil it after pulling these posts free from the intervening ones. Again I experienced the discomfort of dizziness and joined the horse in the shade. The day was certainly warm, but nothing like as unpleasant as it can be in Melbourne or Sydney; and after a little while I returned to work.

Riding home in the dray, I wondered if the dizziness was due to heart trouble. When I was unloading the wire from the dray, the boss sauntered by and remarked:

"You must have found it hot out there to-day."

"Yes, it was so."

"A hundred and twenty-one degrees on the office verandah, anyway," he said.

No wonder I felt dizzy, and no wonder I felt no other discomfort because the humidity must have been almost nil.

Carelessness, accident, and mental instability caused by too much solitude are the three contributors which offer victims to the Spirit of the untamed Australia and compile the great casebook of vanished men.

There is truth in the ancient saying that those whom the gods wish to destroy they first make mad and this god which rules the bush and the plains and the sandhills does precisely that. The human mind, balanced upon the knife-edge between sanity and madness, is so easily dethroned, and it can be and often is dethroned by a thought . . . just one thought expressed with the words 'Where am I?' or 'I'm lost, all right.'

If only, upon realization that one is lost, one would sit down in the shade and remain mentally calm, backtracking in the mind how one arrived at the place, and then calmly decide to play safe and follow one's tracks back to the starting point! But men are often too confident. They decide they have slewed to the right when they ought to have edged to the left, or that they must have misunderstood given directions, and so they attempt to rectify the mistake by what seems to be a short cut, thus taking no heed of time, which in midsummer is so vital.

After the realization that one is lost, comes the attack by panic which swamps out reason and the ability to calculate. Onward one makes to find water, instead of lying down in the darkest available shade until the sun sets. The torment begins shortly after the water-bag is empty. The body burns, and the victim discards his clothes, article by article, even to his boots. His shouts become less and less until he cannot even whisper, and his tongue becomes bigger and bigger until he chokes and drowns in a flood of heat.

There is no tougher section of country in Australia than the great area comprising the north-east quarter of South Australia and bisected by an alleged road known as the Birdsville Track. Watered by a few bores, crossed by empty rivers and creeks, dotted with vast land depressions named lakes, without fences and without roads, the Birdsville Track is often obliterated for miles by drifting sand. Heat, flies and sand; dancing trees and shimmering sandhills; mirage-created Jack's beanstalks which vie in waving drunkenness with the willies of dust that claw the cobalt sky: this is a world as fantastic as the Wonderland which Alice entered.

Mr Arthur Rowland relates that one summer's day when driving down to Marree, he was surprised by the sight of a swagman tramping his way. Naturally, Rowland stopped his car and offered the man a lift. To Rowland's astonishment, the man declined, and, because the nearest bore was some distance away, and the temperature well over the century, he persisted with his offer. The swagman continued to refuse a lift, asserting he was independent of station managers and their cars.

Obviously, Rowland could not use compulsion, and he could not remain with the professional hiker. The meeting occurred a little south of the Cannuwaukaninna Bore. The next bore to the south would be the Dulkaninna Bore, distant about fifteen miles. Having told the swagman how far off was the next water, and having drawn attention to the great heat of the day, Rowland continued his journey, reporting the swagman's presence on the Track at two station homesteads. He returned from Marree a few days later, but did not meet the swagman. No one else ever did.

A story having several similar details is told by Mr. Ken Crombie, who at the time was driving the mail-truck from Birdsville to Marree, a dis-tance of some 330 miles, broken only by calls at the four homesteads along the route. At one of these homesteads he was born and grew to manhood, so that very few, if any, knew the Track and the country better than he.

One of his passengers on this particular trip was a stockman from Glengyle Station who was going down to Marree for a holiday. It was summer, and the temperatures were fairly high. The Track was heavy with drift sand and the average speed but little higher than ten miles an hour at best.

When about half way to Marree, the Glengyle stockman complained that the truck was too rough to ride on and decided he would walk to Marree. He got down at the Mount Gason Bore, and the truck went on. Crombie felt no anxiety and was confident of picking him up again on the return trip to Birdsville.

On the next north-bound trip he did meet the stockman, who was walking along the Track and was quite well and satisfied that walking in the heat was better than riding on a rough truck. He was then a few miles south of Mount Gason itself and about twenty-two miles from the next bore, named Mirramitta.

Three days later Crombie came down once more from Birdsville and, naturally, watched the Track for the stockman's footprints. Eventually he saw them and was able to follow them while driving the truck for some ten miles ... when they vanished. Stopping the truck, he went back along the track, and then found that the stockman had left the barely discernible road and struck away to the south-east, in which direction there was no bore or homestead that side of the New South Wales border.

The heat was bad and the wind was rising, but, nothing daunted, Crombie took a filled waterbag and set off to track down the stockman. For some twelve miles he tracked him over sandhills and across empty lake beds, the mirage hemming him in on all sides, the tormenting flies partially blinding him, the burning sun slashing at his back. The wind gained strength and raised the red sand to blow it along the ground and fill in the lost man's tracks. Twelve miles! After more than three hours' tracking the tracks 'blew out' in the terrible country bordering the Cooper's Creek, and Crombie had to give up and tramp back to the mail truck.

The case was reported to the homesteads and to the police at Marree. A party went out to search the middle reaches of the Cooper. Even the man's bones were never discovered.

ANOTHER man, a dingo-trapper named Hertal Smith, vanished after he left Kalladare homestead to proceed to Kanowana Station, a distance of only 50 miles out. Although a stranger to the country over which he intended to cross, Smith was an experienced bushman, and, too, was equipped with four camels and the usual gear. Before he started he was given plainly rough directions ... to proceed for so many miles to a surface dam which held water, and after leaving the dam to bear away to the right, when he would cut an old track leading to Kanowana.

When he did not reach Kanowana, a search party set out upon his tracks. Smith and his pack camels had reached the surface dam all right, and there camp was made. The next morning, Smith had loaded his camels, and immediately after that operation was completed, or very shortly afterwards, the camels had been frightened by something and all broke away, one being found months afterwards still alive and with the pack-saddle growing into its back.

The search party picked up Smith's tracks at the point of the breakaway, and soon afterwards saw that he had gone on instead of returning to his starting point, which was much nearer to him than his destination. That was his first mistake. His second was to bear away to the left when he had been given to understand without any doubt of it that he had to bear away to the right to cut the old road to Kanowana.

A few miles further on, the party came on Smith's cardigan. That was all they found of him, for his tracks 'blew out' in the vicinity of the Cooper's Creek, which had taken him forever.

Why did Hertal Smith bear away to the left when he was told to bear to the right? Why did the stockman walking to Marree leave the Birdsville Track after following it for ten miles or so? Despite the tales of the romanticists, the mirages wouldn't fool a bush-bred child of five years. Men with but a few years' experience of the Inland are able to steer a rough course by the sun or the stars. The stockman had water with him when he was last seen, and the dingo-trapper would not travel without it even if he had to carry it in a battered jam tin.

Perhaps it was that the stockman, travelling alone for those several days, was attacked by the Bush Spirit's insidious ally named Solitude. Almost certainly, the stockman and Solitude were not strangers, and a man can be out on his horse after cattle or mustering sheep, and now and then be quite unconscious of the pressing outside world whilst he is withdrawn into another world of imagination in which he takes part in an argument or an imaginary scene. I suggest that the stockman on foot to Marree suffered such a withdrawal into that other world, and that, when he came back into the material world about him, he found that his legs had taken him away from the track. And so, believing he would 'cut' the track by heading for a particular compass point, he went forward instead of back-tracking himself to the point where he had left the track. On and on, until the water supply had given out; then panic; then loss of all sense of direction.

As for the experienced dingo-trapper, having been in a similar situation with camels, I can imagine his frame of mind when his camels got way. He would be furiously angry, most likely with himself for giving the camels the chance to break. Such would be his mental state that the idea of going back to his starting point and having to admit the disaster was not to be thought of. No, he would go on to the more distant Kanowana and obtain other camels or packhorses and equipment. He had only to bear away to the left to cut that old road. Forward, then, and not back. Damn the camels! Just that degree of anger to trick his mind into accept-ing the word 'left' for the correct word 'right.' He, too, pressed on and on, and his water gave out and panic triumphed when it was too late to get back to the surface dam.

In 1927, Mr. George Armstrong was riding after cattle across a great land depression named Box-Flat Swamp, when he came upon a curious mound of bones, bleached white. Examination proved the bones to be the skeleton of a man with the skeleton of a dog resting upon it. Identification was impossible, and it could only be assumed that the human skeleton was that of an Afghan who had disappeared several years before while looking for his camels. The Afghan had been accompanied by a dog, which had perished with and upon his master.

Between the flood land of the Diamantina River and that of the Cooper's Creek are a maze of sandhills forty-odd miles across. Among them is no water, and when the wind blows they become a raging inferno of red dust. They are named Dead Men Sandhills, and this is why they were so named.

About the year 1900, in the dry season, four men set off on horses from Coongie Station to attend the races at Birdsville. Their way lay across what afterwards became known as Dead Men Sandhills, where, in the heat and dust, they became 'slewed' in a world that has no horizon. As so often happens to a party under such circumstances, they fell into dissension concerning the way to continue to Birdsville. It ended by one man going forward and three going back to the Cooper's and water.

The man who elected to go on reached the Diamantina, and a water-hole. The three who decided to return never reached the Cooper's Creek. Their remains were discovered some considerable time afterwards. Had they not cut the horses' throats for the blood, they would perhaps have escaped, for killing the horses was about the worst thing they could have done.

A young man did the same thing and perished. He was looking for stock work and on reaching an out-station named Drokley was told that the manager was then at the head station, Coongie. The distance from point to point is forty miles. As in those days there was no telephone communication, and as the young man was told he would most likely be given employment, he decided to ride to Coongie to interview the manager.

A week or so later the manager arrived at the out-station. The young man had not reached Coongie, and a party set out to look for him. They tracked his horse to within five miles of the Cooper's Creek, and water. There the young man had decided he was 'bushed.' His water supply had given out. He killed the animal and drained its blood into a quart-pot, and set off back to the out-station. Had he permitted the horse its head, it might have taken him on to the water, though this is doubtful because the animal was not in its own country.

When Mr Arthur Rowland was managing Innamincka Station, a team of men was putting down a surface dam some considerable distance south of the homestead. The weather was hot, and one of the men rode away in the afternoon to search for strayed bullocks. He did not return that night, and the following morning the mare he had ridden was found back at the camp with her foal. The disappearance was reported to the police at the township of Innamincka.

They went out but failed to find the lost man.

At this time Rowland was away on a cattle muster, and on his return to the homestead he set out with two aboriginal stockmen. Starting from the tank-sinkers' camp, they followed the mare's tracks and eventually came to a tree to which she had been neck-roped. There was the beginning of the tale.

The lost man had decided when darkness fell to camp for the night. During the night, the horse had broken away from the tree and had gone back to her foal at the camp. The next morning, the lost man, who knew the mare had a foal and should have known she would make back to it, set off independently instead of following her tracks. He walked southward into a land where there is no water for many, many miles.

Rowland and his boys tracked him for five days. He had crossed sandhills and dry swamps; on the edge of one he had frantically dug for water with his bare hands. The water in the bags carried by the search party's horses gave out. The only moisture the animals had was contained in a rare patch of green herbage, and when the parched men ate this they suffered severe abdominal pain. To save their own lives they were forced to abandon the search.

The man was never found. The bodies of those taken by the still untamed Australia seldom are.

Bottle hoard at Innamincka Station, as photographed by shearer Jim Cown in 1931 (State Library of South Australia).

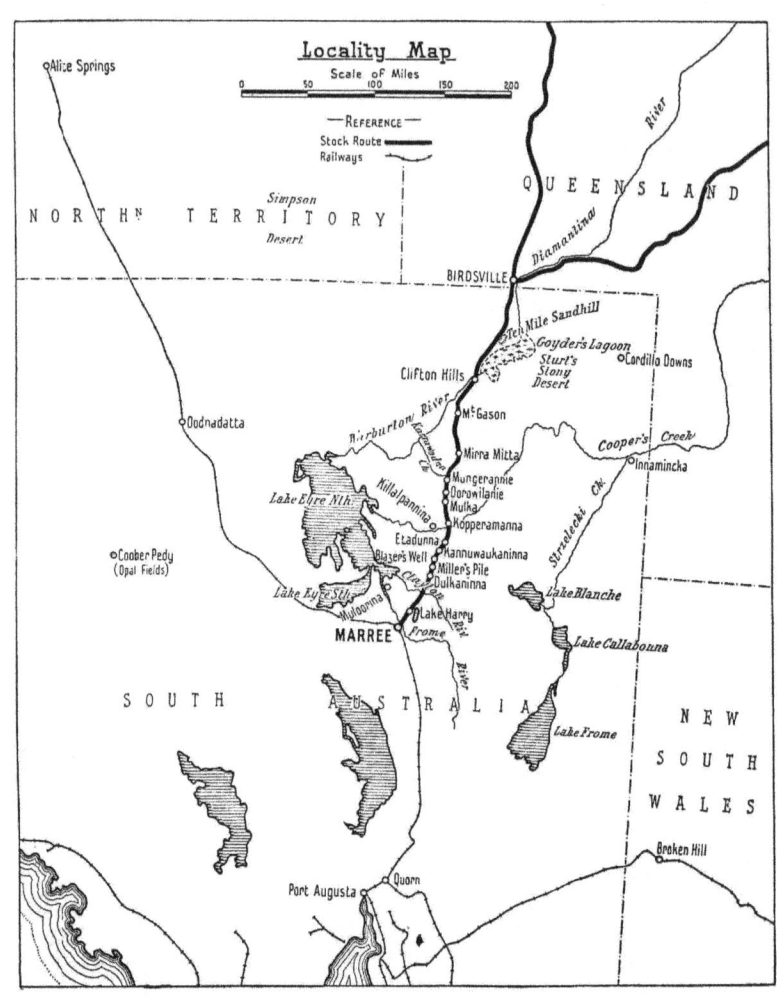

10.

WALKING THE CATTLE

IT'S a place where the almost unbroken horizon is dead level with your horse's hooves, where there is no eye-rest from the spaces of the sky, and there is no obstacle to weaken the wind. Nothing is correctly proportioned. A distant sand dune is like a towering cathedral. Your six feet are dwarfed to eighteen inches.

The place is a gibber plain not far north of Birdsville where the boundaries of States angle in south-western Queensland. The time is early one morning in August. A speckled mass of rebellious animals is being slowly rotated by three riders whose whips now and then "pop" like champagne corks. Quarter of a mile from the milling cattle—it seems less than fifty yards—several horseman are bunched in conference, for this morning the drover is to take over cattle from the Station and move them down the stock route to the railway at Marree.

Two of these horsemen join those with the cattle, and from the rotating wheel a round dozen units are cut from the edge and driven toward the remaining horsemen, who have formed themselves, into a lane, the drover taking position on one side and the station manager on the other. Along the lane are driven the dozen beasts cut from the herd, and after them the herd is permitted to follow in a thin stream. As they pass, the manager and the drover make the tally until the arranged number is reached, when the stream is cut off.

The six hundred which have passed the checkers are taken in charge by the drover's men, the remaining cattle being driven back by the station riders. The details of the drive are then settled. The drover receives the way-bill, a document listing under classifications the breeds, the brands, the sex, and the total number, and signed by the manager on behalf of the owners. At any time a policeman or a stock inspector can demand to be allowed to check the entire herd with the waybill. The laws of the stock route are easy to obey and not easy to circumvent.

The time table is worked out in the rough. By law the cattle must travel a minimum of twelve miles per day, for if they are kept back to graze and travel, say, only five miles per day, they will by that much deprive following herds of feed. The date that the cattle are to reach Marree, some 350 miles to the south, is agreed upon, the manager is to arrange for rail trucks to be in readiness at the trucking yards to convey the beasts to Adelaide.

There is, of course, the subject of finance. The drover in this instance is contracting to deliver the herd for £45 a week, from which he will pay his men five pounds a week and their keep and maintain his plant of forty horses and the considerable saddlery. On him rests all the responsibility, and the life is not without its hazards.

All over Australia, cattle herds are on the move during the winter and spring months. They travel outward from the interior to the railways or to fattening properties near markets. They keep to the defined stock routes like water to river channels, herd after herd flowing down the channels like water freshets. It is estimated that in Australia there are fourteen million cattle.

The Birdsville-Marree stock route, some 330 miles long, is a conduit along which many south-western Queensland herds pass to the Adelaide market. Into it also pour the cattle from the runs adjacent to it; during an average season from six to seven thousand arrive at Marree.

WE are going down with six hundred, plus a few extra for ration meat. They are in good condition, for the rain came early this winter and already the new feed is ripening in the shelter of the sand ranges. The drover is one who appears never to be worried. A big man, he laughs from his stomach upward, and other men, happening to notice the size of his fists, think before they look cross-eyed at him. The cook is elderly and past his bronco-riding days. The horse-tailer is an aboriginal who knows it is nice to get up in the morning but nicer to stay in bed. Andy and Jack are the lads of the bush, fearing nothing on legs and good mouth-organists. The former spends most of his watch at night yodelling, the latter composing poetry and singing it to the cattle.

Men's fashions have changed greatly in these parts, the ensemble comprising the American-type leather jacket, tight-fitting slacks moulded into short leather gaiters, elastic-sided riding boots, and spurs. The condition of the spurs is in accordance with age. In youth you wear a dainty goose-necked affair with the rowels removed and replaced with sixpences to make them ring: in middle age you wear rusty iron, with or without rowels: and later on in life you wear, perhaps, one spur. But no matter what your age, the horses have plenty of sting, and the cattle have plenty of truculence and more stubbornness. Hat fashions haven't altered. They still wear them wide of brim and tall of crown, and they still use them for flailing a horse and lifting dixies off a fire.

All set for the trip, the drover parts from the manager and rides after his cattle, which, despite weather and other conditions, must be delivered into the railway trucks at the time arranged about thirty days hence.

Meanwhile, the cook is preparing camp at the Nine-Mile Creek north of Birdsville and not so far from the flowing Diamantina, which is being reported upon per wireless from many station homesteads.

Drowsing under the creek trees are the cook's six pack-horses, their heavy packs, which contain everything needful, now removed. The fire is going well, and will provide the ashes to cook the damper bread for the morrow. The cook has lopped branches and with them makes a windbreak for sleeping men. As the drovers are unable to enjoy long and uninterrupted sleep, what they get of it is to be obtained in as much comfort as possible, the "possible" being extremely limited.

The stew of diced beef and potatoes is simmering merrily, and the sun has yet to sink from the level of your eyes to the level of your boots, when over a long low rise appear nodules of colour: the Herefords and the Shorthorns and the Aberdeens. For a little while they are silhouetted against the northern sky, and then they come flowing towards the creek with the slow inevitability of the hour hand down a clock face. Away in the sunset the tailer is hobbling all the horses bar those needed for the night watches.

The cattle and their flanking riders advance. The drover has given the order to "Walk 'em," and the beasts move in a compact mass down the slope to the creek in which water lies in narrow holes. Having been given the opportunity to drink, the beasts are pushed up to the southern flat, where a rider is ahead to stop them and so bring them to rest. They stand, tired and fed. Some bellow and paw the ground. Others gaze back toward the compass point from which they have come. Now and then one will move out, to be cradled back again into the herd. They are all a little uneasy, for they are in strange country.

The tailer comes to camp with three night horses, which he saddles and neck-ropes to nearby trees. The bells suspended from the necks of several horses of the mob are infinitely more musical than the cries of the indignant galahs and the bellowing of the cattle. Having prepared a windbreak for himself and laid upon the ground in the lee his swag of blankets within a thick canvas sheet, the aboriginal draws his dinner from the cook and squats beside his swag with his back to the white men.

Now the sun has buried itself in, a sand dune. The light wind is subsiding and the grey dust above the encamped herd is lazy. Fortunately, this first night promises to be fine and quiet. The drover comes in, unsaddles, hobbles and frees his horse. The two younger men continue circling the herd. One of them begins a yodelling song, and he can perform as well as any broadcaster. Hush-A-Bye, Baby! could well be the song, with variations. The purpose is to hush into composure eight-to nine-hundred-pounder babies … six hundred of them.

One lies down, and others follow suit. The water-moistened cud demands attention. Three elect to be "narks," repeatedly attempting to wander and repeatedly turned back into the herd.

In the gloaming, the tailer mounts his horse and rides out to take first watch. The riders come in and let their horses free in hobbles to find their mates. They wash in a hand basin, slick their hair, being young men, as the actors do on the screen, and then, unlike the film actors, squat on their heels while they eat dinner and smoke and yarn afterwards, aided by the camp-fire light. The drover takes up a large butcher's knife and slices through a perfectly baked damper loaf, uttering the time-honoured phrase: "Another sod, so help me Bob!" While they eat, he complains that they eat too much and would surely break any drover. When they have finished he complains that they have not eaten enough, that they must be in love, and how can they expect to keep watch efficiently if they starve themselves nigh to death.

There is no shouting, and no unduly loud laughter. The cook never rattles a dish, or drops one, and when the men carry their swags to the windbreak they never drop them on the ground, because the sound of the impact, as well as the impact itself, will carry to the herd and, perhaps, cause a stampede. Anything may alarm them, particularly a strange noise, and throughout these first nights they are particularly edgy.

The highlight of every cattle story is, of course, the stampede. These happen less often than is generally thought, but every drover experiences and, therefore, dreads them. The direction of a stampede is unpredictable. More than once the drovers' camp has been obliterated, and more than once sleeping men have been out of their blankets and up trees in the space of three seconds. And they have to be stout trees, too, to withstand a pressure of many tons.

The beasts, or most of them, will be lying down. The majority will be asleep, for cattle, like other animals, do sleep. They are apt to dream, even to suffer nightmare, according to the belief of drovers, and drovers are expert authorities on bovine psychology. For every known cause of a stampede there must be ten not so far established. The cattle do it in one action, from lying down to a gallop, without intervening actions of scrambling to their feet and gazing around to ascertain why they are frightened. If the rider on watch happens to be in front of the stampede, he trusts to luck and his horse, and the horse knows enough not to pause.

A hundred riders would fail to stop a stampede. Let 'em go! Get up alongside 'em! Keep your whip going and yell! Try to turn the leaders! Get the herd circling, no matter how great the circumference! Under these circumstances, a man knows how much of a pal his horse can be.

Thunder will start a stampede. So will the ignition of a match in the hand of a silent watcher on a dark night. The rider on watch sings or recites, or argues politics, not for the purpose of entertaining either himself or the cattle but to keep the nervous beasts always aware of his position and presence. In time a herd will look for the companionship of a rider at night, and gain confidence in the unending guardianship.

The length of watches is matter for arrangement, and is dictated chiefly by the number of the crew. The rider coming off watch will call his relief. There is very little romance in droving, and none at night, especially on wet nights and cold.

There was that night of steady rain and a cold biting south wind. The drover came off watch at two o'clock in the morning. On being shaken awake, his relief pulled the canvas sheet down from his face and exclaimed:

"Why! It's raining!"

"D'you reckon? Well, I don't want it in writing," protested the drover, who then proceeded to roll out his blankets within the heavy canvas sheet, unlace and step out of his boots deep in the mud, discard his saturated overcoat, slide himself into his bed, and finally draw the canvas up over his head and fall asleep with the rain drumming on the canvas against his ear.

Doubtless it would have been unwise to speak to the relief of the romance of cattle droving. He rode away in the pitch darkness to locate the herd. He didn't yodel. He didn't even sing to them. He chanted over and over again all the curses employed by the blacks when they point the bone.

The tailer rides out at dawn to locate the horses, unhobble them and bring them closer to camp, then to cut out the horses required for the day's work. After breakfast of beef steak and damper bread, plus jam and tea or coffee, he helps the cook to pack.

Before sun-up, the riders are with the cattle. The herd has moved off, directed to the south and encouraged to fan out so that every beast may have an opportunity to feed as it travels. And so with a rider on either flank and another to push on the laggards, and the tailer and the cook droving the loose horses and the pack-horses, the herd moves along throughout the day.

Come rain, come shine; come wind and dust; come heat and thunder: the herd moves on. Only the mothers find it tough. The calf born on the track is killed, for it cannot keep up with the herd, and the two following nights the mother is roped to prevent her going back for her calf.

For the men life is as tough as a gin's heels, but the air is sweet and the sandhills in the mirage forever call a man on. They *can* go through a day, a week, a month and months, without blistering their hands by constantly thrusting them into pockets for the cash to pay tram and train fares, and for pots and pictures. They *can* have a bank account, or they *can* have a thick wad in a hip pocket when they go to town.

THE cattle camps along a stock route are as indelibly printed on the drover's mind as are the names of stations on the mind of a man living in an outer suburb. The first camp down from Birdsville is at the boundary fence separating South Australia from Queensland. It was once a vermin fence, but was abandoned for reasons unworthy of discussion. Along the river flats and across the wider flats a few posts remain standing, and most of the netting lies on the ground, too old and rotted to be of service to anyone. Farther out, the sand has at last triumphed, burying long stretches. Then comes Dickeree Camp, with water nearby, and Pandy Pandy Swamp; here there is often water, with feed about the adjacent sandhills. The first good camp is twenty-eight miles from Birdsville, a fine waterhole half-a-mile long, a hundred yards wide, and almost permanently supplied by the Diamantina. Magnificent box and bean trees, beloved by the birds, line the banks.

From this camp the route leaves the Diamantina country for a spell, to cross a seemingly endless succession of sand-ranges running for many miles north-west to south-east and divided by wide flats bearing herbage. Along the lower slopes of the ranges at this time grow new buckbush and other shrubs and masses of herbage which toss into the sunlight a variety of flowers. The farther south, the better the feed.

The Dead Heart! It would be a good thing for the Commonwealth Parliament to pass an act making it a criminal offence for a writer to refer to the Interior of Australia as the Dead Heart. Such a phrase is a gross libel. Never at any time has it been true, and the country's reputation should be safeguarded in law as is the reputation of its citizens.

In a dry year patches of the country will be denuded of vegetation, but nowhere in Australia is there a permanent desert like the Sahara, which no one thinks to call the Dead Heart of Africa. Parts of Australia sometimes fall asleep, but they are not dead. The Heart of Australia continues to pulsate with astonishing vigour.

Grass waving like green wheat. Square miles of springing herbage. Flowers of yellow and of mauve, of blue and pink and red, making a carpet for cattle to walk upon. Even when the rains have failed in one year, or even in two years, the shrubs and the tougher grasses will provide sustenance for travelling stock.

The sand-ranges are like great ocean waves preceding a storm. The cones smoke like volcanoes, hinting at what these ranges will do when a strong wind is allied to hot sunlight. The herd is pushed through Lovers' Nook, a gully between monstrous sandhills, and on and over the lesser ranges of red and golden sand.

The choice of night camps is dependent on the availability of water. If the drover could have it all his way, he would have good feed growing between camps rather than about the camps, so that his cattle would arrive at night camp well fed and content to lie down and attend to cud. Hungry cattle camp badly.

Our six hundred arrive at the night camps with the timing of a train arriving at suburban stations. The herd, fed and tired, is willing to camp, to sleep and dream, to listen to the yodeller and the poet singing his verses on Yandama Bill, The Bullocky, The Queen of Marree, and The Wedding of Dan MacGee. What names these camps possess — Ten-Mile Waterhole (ten miles from where nobody knows), Andrewilla Waterhole, Little Pelican Hole, Bert's Hole!

After Bert's Hole the cattle have to cross the hungry, 30-miles-wide Diamantina. There is barely enough feed on this belt of unfertile land to sustain a goat, and after an inch of rain it is soft enough to bog a duck. Miles separate narrow, winding, empty channels which appear like those dug by men with horse-scoops. The thirty miles are as flat as a board, and yet you cannot see farther than a mile. The land seems to rise upon all sides, but it doesn't. It is as though the herd is carried over in the bottom of a shallow basin. A line of miserable cane- grass clumps appear, at a distance, like enormous grasshoppers. To view the cattle in close formation from a point a quarter of a mile away is to see a prehistoric reptile wallowing in the grey mud, and when the drover raises his arm to signal "Walk 'em, boys!" he looks like the Statue of Liberty astride a beetle.

WHEN the mirage has finished playing the fool with the sand dunes marking the confluence of the rivers, the only remaining sign-post is the sun. You see lines of gum trees far ahead which turn out to be clumps of canegrass, and the mirage tricks you a dozen times before you see the real trees bordering Goyder's Lagoon on the southern shore.

Thus pass the hours and the days. Many of the beasts want to lie down as they have been accustomed to do when free on the station. The herd will not move of itself; it has to be driven and kept on its course at a regulated speed. On some days the wind is as keen as a knife, on others warm and full of the promise of summer's heat. The rain clouds will sweep in from the nor'-west, and the thunder clouds will pile into mountains of ice and threaten a bad night with frightened cattle.

Big Lagoon Waterhole is a picnic ground for kangaroos, and an ideal place for a naturalist's honeymoon: soft and shadowed and peopled with birds. Old Lagoon Waterhole, situated on a treeless plain, would frighten casual explorers if left there for a week to admire the lack of scenery in company with the silence. One must live for a long time in this country to feel the distances and understand the moods of the sky and the haunting winds.

There are people living at the Seven-Mile Bore now that the homestead of Clifton Hills is established there. It is the first house, and they are the first people one has seen since leaving Birdsville, one hundred miles to the north. We haven't come to a fence—yet.

A few miles south of the homestead the gibber plain dips down to sandy country and the way lies across Beefwood Creek, which runs through Potato Tin Sandhills, where the flowers grow in great bunches.

The cook has run out of meat, and just before the herd reaches camp, the riders cut out half-a-dozen beasts and drive them to the trees. One of the trees contains the drover, who drops a beast with a rifle bullet. The others are sent back to the herd, and the killed beast is stripped of its hide and great slabs of meat are cut away and laid upon a bed of gum tips to firm in the night air. Most of the meat is salted.

Kidman's Swamp, next on our route, keeps evergreen the name of a great Australian. The next night camp is among The Seven Sisters, where is the Ultoornurra Waterhole, which anyone can own so far as I care. It takes a couple of hours to move the herd up the long rise to Mount Gason Bore, and two more to travel them down the far side to skirt Mount Gason itself. It was here that a sand storm overwhelmed a drover and his cattle. The wind blew the men off their horses. The sand blotted out the daylight for two days and the star-sheen for two nights. When a few of the horses were found, all the mustering over a period of weeks failed to locate one hundred of the cattle.

The Eight-Mile Creek runs between high plains, and at the southern edge of one there can be seen the Mitta Mitta Bore and the skeleton of the house which once was a store at which could be bought almost anything. A little distance away there is a grave surrounded by a pole fence; the poles had to be carted for miles, as, indeed, had the wood with which to cook. The widow lived on alone. She would not be persuaded to leave. The mail passed northward one week and southward the next week. Ten or a dozen droving plants might pass by during the winter months; during the summer no one came excepting the mailman. Silence is a bad companion. Now Silence is all that is left.

THE high plains are apt to make you humble, make you feel no larger than a cockroach, and not so very different. The camp at Karawadna Creek is appreciated, although the country bordering it is as poor as a blackfellow's dog. The country is very different through the Mungerannie Gap, a devil's punchbowl where flourish bluebush and saltbush, and the creeks are lined with robust scrub trees. All is green and inviting beneath the blue of the sky resting upon the table-topped hills. It's the place for a Ned Kelly, or a Two-Gun Jackson, stage-coach hold up—with nothing missing.

The freshest of beef flows on over the sand dunes back of Mungerannie Homestead, where the drover calls for wireless news. The next night camp is at Euralina, the aboriginal name surely being that of a flower or a favourite lubra. Next comes Apattoonganie Wells, and from here the herd is pushed across the terrific sandhills bordering Cooper's Creek, where there is a depression now filled with water and edged with herbage.

In contradistinction to the bare Diamantina plain, the Cooper was once shaded by flourishing box-trees. The trees are dead—thousands upon thousands of trees killed by the droughts in the Twenties. The trees of this Dead Forest are stark and grey, and here you feel the ghosts of bygone peoples. The cattle are nervous, too, and it is good to arrive at Salt-bush Pan amid the golden sandhills skirting the great plain in the centre of which is Cannu—wauk—an—inna Bore. After this plain, the sand-ridges flank the way to Blazer's Well, with its windmill and nearby stockman's hut where live no stockmen.

Dulkaninna Bore steams hot and gives one million gallons every twenty-four hours, and here the cattle are offered a drink because there is no water at the next camp, Big Sandy Hill. The reward for the dry night is provided by the Clayton Bore, which flows down the bed of a wide creek bordered by leafy gums and edged with tall reeds among which pipe the water hens and the ducks salute the solemn ibis and the stately crane.

Only a few more days of pushing on the plodding beasts, only a few more nights of keeping watch over the resting herd. The summit of a long rise presents Lake Harry and the Nor-East Cliff, a land depression extending beyond the mirage - hidden horizon to the east, with, beyond its south-western edge, the long flat-topped hills burned to henna by the summer suns.

The feeling is that the herd will never reach the Nor-East Cliff, but eventually they pass through a gap, to come out at Lake Harry Homestead, where there is a bore with a grove of date-palms. After watering beside the palms, the herd is moved on to the dry camp at Salt Bushes, and thence to Dry Well for the last night out from Marree.

THREE hundred and fifty miles this herd has travelled in about thirty-odd days. The distance is not great compared with other routes out from the Territory. This season the Birdsville Track bloomed with flowers and sparkled with water. But it can be rough, the roughest stock route in Australia, bar none. And yet in one exceptionally bad year a drover contracted to deliver cattle to the yards at Marree. The country was so poor that he had to employ an Afghan with camels to pack chaff for the horses and water from bore to bore. He brought the herd into Marree, without losing a beast.

On the gibber plain outside the town the drover and his riders cut and draft the light beasts from the heavier animals, and in two small divisions the herd is yarded with the aid of cracking whips and much shouting by men whose release from constant duty is at hand. From the yards the beasts are driven into the trucks, the drafting ensuring that the light beasts will not be injured by the heavy animals.

When the last beast is entrained, the job is done. The drovers make camp in a town yard. The horses are belled and hobbled and loosed on the plain, the tailer's horse being retained and chaff-fed. No camp fire is required. What! Eat steak or beef stew off tin plates, and thick slices of butterless damper bread, when at the Hotel there awaits a dinner of roast meat and green vegetables served on real china plates, and tea from real china cups resting on saucers? Plus a fruit pie with cream, and a real live girl to wait on you! Have a heart!

And afterwards you hear an engine whistle and you go out to watch the rake of cattle trucks pass through the station. And long after that you may hear the rumble of the train crossing the plain south of Marree, and remember those star-lit nights you rode round the herd.

Japanese and Malay pearl divers off Broome about 1928.

11.

PEARLING TOWN OF THE NORTH-WEST

THERE once were six hotels in Broome, and something like 3,000 people to keep the bar tenders busy, but with the decline of population three went out of business.

Nowadays the "Roebuc," the "Continental" and the "Governor Broome" manage quite well to serve eight hundred people. There may once have been narrow alleys crowded with Eastern life, and bag camps lining the foreshore, but now there are only ugly iron shacks and weathered bungalows, and large flap-clapping iron buildings into which, in past days, the gleaming pearl shell was poured to be classified and packed for export.

How Broome came to be founded on the tongue of land jutting into Roebuc Bay none can tell. Without doubt the haven provided by the Dampier Creek was used by the Malay voyagers long before Dampier saw the coast. A certain Lieutenant Helpman reported shell in 1851, but as the official records were not begun until 1870, there is a blank of twenty years.

There are three gateways to Broome: by sea, by air, and by road. Each gate provides a sharp and distinctly different first impression of this shopless township which is akin to a semi-formed outer suburb of an inland mining centre. Broome was never intended to be entered through the land gate, for it is a place having its genesis in rough bough sheds built at the edge of mangrove swamps. As it could not grow seaward, of necessity it had to expand over the coast sand dunes and occupy the flat land within the arm of the Dampier Creek. There being much flat land, the men who came to trade in pearls and shell, boats and gear and foodstuffs, appeared to build as far from each other as possible. Doubtless the wealth garnered from the sea by the brown man and the black man made them inordinately suspicious of each other. Thus, by the land gate you enter Broome by the back door.

Were it not for the adventurous coloured men, Broome might never have become a township, and most certainly would never have become famous. White men will adventure, but comparatively few are physically able to stand up to work at fathoms deep in sea water, and until the brown man is encouraged to return Broome will languish in its tepid climate. Without the oyster shell there would be no reason for its continued existence, and shell cannot be harvested without divers to raise it from the sea floor, and without boats to convey the divers to their work and to bring the shell to land.

Once, there were three hundred luggers based on Broome, and these boats "fished" as far south as Port Hedland and as far north as Darwin. Even in the last year of peace before World War II there were 181 boats in northern Australian waters. Today there are but twenty-two luggers, and many of these are operating with defective equipment, replacements being impossible. There used to be two thousand brown men engaged in the industry— Malays, Phillipinos, Koepangers and Japanese. Even in 1938-39 there were 1,750. There are now less than two hundred, and some of these are being deported.

What is really an extraordinary situation is that while men and boats are at an all-time "low," the price of pearl shell is at an all-time "high." I watched brown men bringing off a lugger long sacks each containing two-and-a-half hundredweight of shell. The contents of each sack were worth £68.15 in Australian currency, or some two hundred and twenty of those magical monetary units called dollars, of which it is said we are so short. I saw wood cases packed with shell, and on each were stencilled the words 'NEW YORK.' All the shell goes to America, and for every ton of it America pays 1,750 odd dollars . . . and cannot get enough.

Five hundred and fifty pounds Australian per ton! In the mid-thirties the price was a mere £100 per ton. The value of pearl shell production in Australia is set down at over £11,000,000 up to the year 1940.

Diver Omar Kinang was located at one of the hotels. He is small and dapper, round of head and olive of complexion, having a small dark moustache and twinkling black eyes.

We wanted to watch a diver at work. We wanted to see his lugger. We understood that he was sailing that afternoon. "Be on the beach at two o'clock. You go aboard from the beach and I put you off at the jetty across the bay. Go down! All right, I'll go down for you. Be on time . . . please. Tide will catch us if we're late."

We were waiting on the beach before the hour named. Little waves came in between the headlands formed by the mangroves beyond which two luggers lay at anchor. There were pearly clouds beneath the sun, and long fingers of pale gold lancing down the skyway to touch the seaward horizon. The sea was the colour of pearl shell, and it had the soft satiny sheen of pearls.

There came to join us an Indonesian. He wore a raincoat, and he carried a neat suitcase. He might have been a university lecturer. He could have been a lawyer or a doctor. He was, in fact, a number two diver. Omar came down to the beach, spoke softly to the grave Indonesian, and departed. Two Malays arrived, bringing bread and other foodstuffs. From one of the distant luggers came a dinghy, pushed forward by oars in the hands of a tall and deceptively solemn Australian aboriginal. We all boarded his dinghy and were conveyed to a lugger designated B2 and painted green with white upper works. The deck was crowded with gear and several of the crew who had preceded us.

The laughter was infectious. An infant ran up the rigging, and the aboriginal told me proudly that the infant was his son and that he, the parent, was named Raphael Phillips and could speak thirteen languages in addition to good English. His sense of humour was as deep as the sea and as wide as his knowledge of the sea.

There was laughter and shouting and a babel of orders. One man went below to the galley, he having been appointed cook for the day. Another dropped down into the engine room and proceeded to manhandle the eighteen-horsepower kerosene engine. The engine began to cough and grunt. Three men ran for'ard and winched up the anchor. Raphael Phillips, who appeared to be the captain, shouted an order, and up went the mainsail to catch the light breeze.

With the sail to assist the complaining engine, the lugger slid of the mud into deep water, just in time to escape on the ebbing tide. The craft moved slowly out into Roebuc Bay, and there lay Broome, a cluster of iron roofs beyond the salmon-coloured sand dunes. To the northward jutted the long and high jetty, and beyond it, the line of coastal dunes broken here and there, with white buildings nestling in the breaks. The sea in the bay was an iridescent green, the light-green of a marlin on being taken from the water, the light-green of opal; and when the gulls flew by, their breasts and under wings caught and held the exact colour of the sea.

Far to the south, a tongue of brilliant red land appeared to be eagerly reaching across the Indian Ocean towards Africa. From the tip of this land marking the southern extremity of Roebuc Bay, there arose three straight columns of smoke, and whilst I wondered what those smokes might mean Raphael Phillips came to stand with me. Where those smokes rose from the red land there he had been born. As a boy he had come to Broome to be educated at the Spanish convent school, and as a young man he had begun to live at sea and to follow the shell beds up and down the endless coast. His voice was soft, and behind the humorous front was pride, pride in being able to speak thirteen languages and pride in being the father of the imp perched at the masthead.

Passing Buckley Rock to starboard, we sailed into the open bay. There was no swell. The colour of the sea changed to silver-grey, as did the breasts and wings of the gulls that followed us. The vivid green mangrove masking Dampier Creek drew back to give a better view of Broome beyond the sea-gate, a township guarded from the wind that comes hurtling down from the nor'west by those low salmon-tinted dunes.

Off the jetty we were hoved to while Raphael Phillips rowed the dinghy to bring off Diver Kinang and his wife and baby son. We who expected to be put ashore at the jetty were kept on board. The diver came aboard with agility, and all hands welcomed his wife and the baby, especially the baby.

The normal trip for a shell cruise is six weeks, and during this period from port the "tucker boat" keeps in touch with all the schooners at sea and delivers fresh meat and vegetables. The best shell grounds are south of Broome and off the Ninety-Mile Beach at a depth of about twelve fathoms.

MASKED Mrs Kinang what she thought about her husband's work, and did her husband think of making his son a diver. They laughed, both of them, at the preposterous idea, and Mrs Kinang told me that she would be much happier when her husband gave it up.

"Don't believe any of the thrilling tales about divers being attacked by great sharks and things like that," Mrs Kinang urged me. "It's not the big things but the little ones that can be so bad. Omar went down one day when the face glass of his helmet wasn't screwed in properly, and he was nearly drowned before they got him up. Then another time, towards the end of a day's work, a small shark swam round him. It could be easily frightened away by Omar releasing air, but he thought that a nice little shark would make a fine fish tea, and he grabbed at it. It twisted and fastened on the arm of his suit and tore it open, letting in the water. Anything can happen, you know. They get so careless, and so do the tenders."

"What of the giant gropers said to swallow a man?" I asked. "And what of the giant clams said to hold fast upon the foot of an unwary diver?"

"Air bubbles for the groper," Omar contributed, stepping into the diving suit, "the unwary diver doesn't last long. As the wife said, it's the little things . . . like the stone fish."

Omar had emerged from the cabin wearing white woollen stockings reaching to his groin, and a heavy woollen sweater. The second diver, Baharon Ali was similarly arrayed against the cold, and having stepped into the cumbersome under-water costume each sat on a chair on either side of the hatch while tenders secured to their feet the great lead-soled boots.

"Stone fish?" I echoed, and Omar's wife glanced at me, her lips compressed.

"They're the worst excepting the stingrays," she told me. "The stone fish cling to the shell, and they are the same colour and hard to distinguish. The diver doesn't wear gloves, and when picking up the shell his hand can come into contact with a stone fish. The effect of the sting is dreadful. It'll make a man scream, and presently send him into convulsions and kill him."

"There's no antidote?"

"Oh, yes," she said surprisingly—surprisingly, since most books say there is no antidote. "They've discovered an antidote. When the diver is stung, he holds on to the fish and signals to be hauled up. When he is brought to the surface, the tender takes the stone fish from him, gouges out the fish's eyes and allows the fluid from the eye-sockets to fall on the place stung. The antidote, they say, will work in less than half an hour. If he doesn't bring up the fish, then there's only morphia that will relieve the pain a little."

"And a full bottle of brandy," supplemented Omar.

"Brandy," Mrs Kinang went on. "They never eat at the beginning of the day's work below. Coffee laced with brandy for breakfast, and more coffee and brandy when they come up for a spell. Then a big meal at the end of the day. If they go below on a full stomach they have cramps and other pains." She laughed, softly. "Omar is growing thin. At the beginning of the season they go off fat and jolly. At the end of it they come home as skinny as an old rooster. I'll be glad when Omar gives up."

"The annual lay-up is from December to March, I understand. That's the bad season, isn't it?" I prompted.

"They are the months of the blows . . . the willies. No one goes to sea at that time. Sometimes a blow will come out of season, and they know when it's coming, too, long before the barometer tells them, or the wireless. When the divers are working below and they see the weed moving slowly backward and then forward like grass in the wind, that's a sure sign of a "cock-eyed bob," as some people call them. Then it's inboard and away to shelter at some place. Bring me up a pearl, Omar."

OMAR Kinang smiled, nodded to his wife, and kept his head motionless while his tender lowered the round helmet down to the iron collar of the rubber corsage. The slightly built agile man was transformed into a grotesque monster. The tender proceeded to bolt the helmet to the collar, using a wrench. Baharon became similarly transformed, and then both divers were assisted to their ungainly feet and taken to one and the other side of the boat, where short iron ladders went down into the water.

There they paused. Omar was saying something jocular as the round face piece was screwed into the front of his helmet. The air hose was screwed to the back of the helmet, and the life-line clipped to the breast plate. Over the low gunwales they clambered, feeling with their heavy boots for the rungs of the ladder, each taking with him a light metal shell basket.

The tenders were ready to pay out life-line and hose. The divers tested the air inside their now sealed helmets. I could hear air escaping when their puny hands touched a valve. And then they stepped down deeper into the sea, appeared to lie back into the water and slowly sank.

I saw a whitish shape pass slowly along my side of the lugger. Below surface it appeared like a shark, belly upward. The shape passed away to the stern, vanishing in the slight wake of the boat. The boat is kept gently moving forward while the men are down. Thereafter, I watched the bubbles bursting, two sets of bubbles; and my mind's eye followed those two men down and down into the green depths, and saw them looking below themselves as they neared the sea's floor, making sure they did not land on a stingray. The bubbles informed us when they touched bottom. Then the sets drew closer, and one set of bubbles followed the other set, one diver, probably Baharon, following the other. I could follow all their movements on the sea-bed as they worked for shell . . . just to show two strangers in Broome how it is done.

Raphael Phillips and another man now stood in the stern, each holding in his hands the life of a man, each waiting for signals to come up the life-line. Raphael watched the bubbles, watched the men working the air pumps, watched other members of the crew at their respective stations, watched the sky and the sea. There was no jest, no laughter.

"A good diver will send up from 90 to 112 pounds of shell on one shift," Mrs Kinang was telling me as I watched the two sets of bubbles. "During a good season, from late March to late November or early December, he will earn something up to £1,000. The average earnings are around £700, and at £700 he has to fork out £125 in taxation."

The twin sets of bubbles drew farther aft. Raphael Phillips noted the coloured ribbons threaded through the life-line, and Mrs Kinang told me that the ribbons set at intervals enabled the tenders to know exactly how far away their charges were at any given moment. How far distant, how far deep, for depth is known by the leadline.

"How long has your husband been diving?" I asked Omar's wife, and she replied that he had been down off the Australian coast at least two thousand times. She had always hated the thought of his going below, but he liked the adventure of it, and the gamble of it, too, for down in those cold green aisles of the sea had been found the "Star of the West," a pearl almost as large as a sparrow's egg and worth £14,000. Where that pearl came from another of equal splendour might go up in an oyster shell from Omar to the shell opener. Pearls belong to the divers, in most cases—they are the lucky Chance.

"They're coming up," announced Mrs Kinang.

The tenders now reminded me of handline fishermen as they hauled in their catch. I saw one "fish," as it neared the surface, being drawn after the boat, and then along the side of the boat to surface close by the ladder. The diver floundered helplessly and was drawn to the ladder, lifted so that he was able to get his great boots on the lowest rung, assisted by the taut life-line to climb the ladder and over the gunwale to the deck.

When tenders had removed the face glass from the men's helmets, it seemed fantastic to observe the human faces deep within the iron spheres, and those faces widened by a smile. Laughter and quip broke loose from the crew as the divers were undressed and the gear carefully stowed. Omar shouted, and a Malay dropped down into the cabin and proceeded to pass up bottles of beer that Omar Kinang might entertain his guests.

The sun was westering and sending down golden bars to point at Broome. The schooner was turned about and headed for the jetty, so far distant that it could not be distinguished from the coastline. The cook served "chow" to delight an epicure. Raphael Phillips's boy came down from the masthead, a mouse attracted to roasted cheese, and Omar managed to eat his ration while nursing his son. He had actually deferred the six-weeks trip by one day that he might entertain us.

Subsequently I found Christopher Brian Taylor who was born in Broome of a West Indian father. He was handling the shell brought up from the sea by Omar Kinang and Baharon Ali, and those other twenty divers working off the coast of Western Australia. He was working in a large shed near the store, and he was surrounded by heaps of gleaming pearl shell and bags containing more shell, and wooden cases into which he was packing shell. Two men were sorting shell from a heap, tossing each piece into one of five floor bins, thus grading the shell into extra heavy, heavy, medium, small, and "chicken."

I watched Brian Taylor packing shell for America, his long fingers reminding me of those of a fur dealer who loved the touch of fur. Taylor's long fingers loved the silky caress of pearl shell, and, without apparent haste, they packed the shell as though they were packing priceless crystal. How many tons had he despatched to the great markets of the world? That he could not answer, for he has been packing shell for many years. But the year books say that in the fiscal year 1938-39 just over 2,600 tons, worth £A244,266 were exported.

I FOUND Captain Hensen at the "Governor Broome," and he presented me to a little old man who once had owned three luggers and had given them away when the Japs were expected at Port Hedland.

"Now we can't get boats, any kind of boats," remarked Captain Hensen. "There's a lugger here that cost £350 to build and fit, and now she's worth £2,500, and she isn't a good craft, either. Still, at £2,500 a boat would pay for itself in a season, perhaps two. Can't obtain the timber to build boats. Can't buy the engines, or the sails. And we can't get the divers. Won't let 'em into the country. They're yelling for increased exports to hard currency countries, and they seem to do everything to hinder us buying or building boats, and they won't let in the divers to go down after the dollars. This season, and now it's August, only sixty tons of shell have been shipped away. There's ninety tons waiting to be shipped. At the end of the season, in December, West Australia might be able to export a total of four hundred tons. That'll mean £220,000 Australian. It's not much in view of the shell that's now maturing along the beds."

Broome will make a come-back when new boats can be built, and when the brown men are invited to return, provided, of course, that if and when that comes about the price of pearl shell is not again down to £100 per ton. Opportunity has been represented as an old man, quite bald but having a long beard. You can grasp him by the beard as he passes, but after he has passed there is nothing left by which to grasp him.

12.

THE VERMIN FENCES
OF WESTERN AUSTRALIA

A PROBLEM of major importance to Australia is adequate protection of the pastoral and agricultural districts against the depredations of migratory animals and the wingless bird, the emu. Non-migratory animals and pests can be dealt with by local action, but without defensive measures undertaken by Government local action is useless against animals which arrive in waves from the outer and unsettled areas deep in the interior of the continent. The problem is greater even than that of erosion, for it is a paramount cause of erosion.

When it is recalled that the area of Australia is three million square miles, that the producing areas lie along the outside edge, and that there are no permanent rivers and mountain ranges rising high above the snow line forming protective barriers, it will be understood that the problem is really national in importance.

Brer Rabbit, who thrives and multiplies under the ideal conditions encountered in Australia, has received much publicity. He has been rightfully blamed for his share in causing erosion as well as reducing the value of pastures on which there is no erosion. A colony of rabbits may be wiped out with fumigants, with traps, and even with shovels, but a migrating rabbit host cannot be so dealt with. Migrating rabbits do not live in burrows —they have left burrows to migrate— and when they do decide to "shift camp" because they have eaten out the country, nothing will stop them excepting a wide river, a very high mountain range, or wire netting. As there are neither rivers nor mountains to bar our rabbits, there is left only wire netting built into fences.

A rabbit migration does not follow a pre-destined route as do rats and other animals in other countries. One pair of rabbits which have burrowed in country where no rabbits have been seen for years will, in the space of one good climatic season, produce a colony of many hundreds. In the space of a second good season the colony will have produced chains of colonies growing outward from the first like the spokes of a wheel. The third year may or may not be a good year, but by then the colonies have become a host so great that the burrows are choked to the entry holes with rabbits. Now the young buck rabbits will be banished from the burrows by the old ones, and they become strong bush rabbits and eventually the leaders of the migration. A migration begins at any moment. I saw one begin.

I saw the bush rabbits sitting up and scenting the air. It was early one morning. It was impossible to count the rabbits within sight. They could scent the rain which had fallen fifty, a hundred miles away. In the late afternoon they began the migration. During the evening I watched them leaving—all making to the north-east. They passed my stockman's hut in ragged array but with a kind of irresistible momentum as awe-inspiring as an avalanche. The next morning there was not a rabbit to be seen.

Because Australia is so large, and because all of it is never affected by drought at the same time, the rabbits when migrating make direct to the rain-refreshed country, which can be at any point of the compass from their original home. They do not run and run until they drop dead with exhaustion. They subsist on gum leaves, shallow roots, tree bark, and, when not halted by wire- netted fences, they may migrate for incredible distances.

The general rule is for waves of rabbits to migrate from the central districts of Australia outward to the coastal districts, but the exceptions to this general rule are many. The Government of New South Wales built a rabbit-and-dingo-proof fence all along its frontier with South Australia. The purpose was to keep outside of New South Wales migrations of rabbits and dogs beginning in South Australia.

One rabbit migration ending at this barrier left a line of casualties forty miles long, a yard wide and two feet deep. That host was halted by the fence on its west side, its South Australian side. I saw a similar migration end at the east or New South Wales side, so that this fence then actually protected South Australia from New South Wales' rabbits. The idea that a netted fence is built to keep something outside is erroneous, for it will also keep something inside; and the sun is no respecter of States and will kill animals on either side a netted fence. Animals that have arrived at such a barrier continue to be imbued with the urge to find a way through it until stricken by the sun.

When the hunting gentlemen of the pioneering days introduced the fox, because the native kangaroo was too agile for the common foxhound, they could not foresee what was in store for the future pastoralists and their sheep. The fox also found here most ideal conditions. The rabbits provided all the food he needed, and there was unlimited scope for him to clear right away from the huntsmen and eat as much as he wished and breed as fast as he could.

At the time when the writer was first working in western New South Wales there were no foxes west of the Darling River. At that time they were to be seen on the eastern bank, having arrived at that point westward. A year or so later the river ceased to run, and they crossed the bed and fed well in the larder provided by the native bush turkey and other ground-nesting birds. To-day, turkeys are seldom seen. But the rabbits remain, and wherever they are, so too are the foxes. It is when the rabbits migrate, or die out through disease, that the fox turns to the young lambs for subsistence.

This applies, fortunately in slightly lesser degree, to the native dingo and the wild dog. Wherever food is plentiful, there will be abnormal increase in animals and birds who live on meat.

On gold first being discovered in Western Australia there were no rabbits in that State. The first rabbits introduced into Western Australia were transported by the teamsters who drove their bullock wagons across the Nullarbor Plain and the Hampton Tableland to seek fortune on the new goldfields. The rodents were released at favoured places "to provide the poor man with meat." Ironically, one of these teamsters subsequently obtained a contract to erect a section of the great Number One Rabbit Fence built by the Western Australian Government right across the State from the south to the north coasts.

However, before the transported rabbits increased to become a menace it was said that a man rode into Coolgardie shouting that the rabbits were coming westward "in millions" and that behind them "followed the dingoes." Coolgardie boasted of its racecourse with its well-kept lawns. A few nights later the lawns disappeared.

The State Government acted with commendable promptitude. It rushed men and materials by rail to Burracoppin, about 170 miles ahead of the advancing rabbits, and constructed the fence which is known as the longest netted fence in the world. From Burracoppin the fence was taken southward to the Southern Ocean and northward to the Pacific, an overall distance of 1,154 miles, thus providing protection not only for the mixed farming areas footing the Darling Range but also to hundreds of thousands of acres of good wheat land subsequently taken up by gold-miners when goldmining became a science.

Thereafter this Number One Fence was to halt waves of migrating rabbits with their camp followers, the wild dog and the fox, and the emu whose migrations are more habitual. These migrating waves began in the eastern States of Australia, and they were not continuous in their action. The wave rises and rolls forward for many miles, slowly subsiding with the advance, pausing for a year or two to gather strength to race onward again. The rabbits which reached the Number One Fence in Western Australia were most likely the great-grandchildren of the rabbits in the first wave surge, but ten times more numerous.

It was unfortunately necessary to construct gateways in this netted barrier of more than a thousand miles to enable road traffic to pass through, and then arose a problem which has remained insoluble—that of gaining complete cooperation of road-users to close the gates.

A vermin fence is not a vermin fence when someone leaves a gate open all night, no matter if the fence is one mile or a thousand miles in length. Despite notices attached to gates requesting travellers to shut them, despite prosecutions for failing to shut the gates, there has always been that minority who, either because of ignorance or that inferiority complex which must express itself by being "agin the Government," persisted in not closing the gates.

I have myself more than once arrived at a gate left open, and have seen the ground massed with the tracks of emus and rabbits passing through the gateway from the virgin country into the settled country. At one such gate I was met by a farmer who belligerently argued against the efficiency of the barrier; even when the tracks of the vermin were pointed out to him he remained unconvinced.

Through the open gateways, and a section of the fence sometimes destroyed by fire, the rabbits eventually gained access to country westward of the barrier stretching from ocean to ocean across Australia's largest State. Thereupon a second fence was constructed approximately one hundred miles westward of the first, running north from the sea at Point Anne, passing through the township of Cunderdin, and finally taking a right turn to meet the Number One Fence at a place known as Gum Creek—a distance overall of 724 miles. Finally, a third fence of 171 miles in length was built from the Number Two Fence, about thirty miles north of Yalgoo westward to the coast at Ajana, north of Northampton. Thus were enclosed from the east and from the north all the agricultural districts of the State, and these barriers kept the rabbits from reaching the southwest corner for thirty years and still enable landholders to keep them in check.

From 1928 to 1931 the writer was employed patrolling a section of 200 miles of the Number One Fence. In those faraway days conditions were very tough, especially through the summer. For administrative purposes the Number One Fence was divided—from Lake Nabberu northward, with headquarters at Jigalong, and southward with headquarters at Burracoppin. On balance, conditions for men patrolling both sections were about level. Those on the northern section were particularly rough, but there men travelled in pairs. On the southern section the conditions were slightly easier, but there men travelled alone, and were not likely to see another human being for a fortnight at a stretch. One has to be singularly equipped mentally to stand that for long; and men came and departed after one trip, and others came and stayed for years—men who loved independence and hated to work under the eye of a boss.

AS stated, those patrolling this southern section worked alone. Only the late Sub-Inspector Coleman was provided with motor transport to oversee his four men and his 700-miles section of fence. The men had to deal with fractious camels harnessed tandem-wise to a heavy drayhaving a high canopy which provided a house on wheels. There was a slight chance of coming out with a severe injury, with the summer shade temperatures ranging between 100° and 115°, the watering places many miles distant, and very few travellers chancing prosecution for using the Government track beside the fence. A broken leg or a torn arm, an axe cut or a snake bite, was something not to be thought of.

Nowadays the patrol men travel in pairs and use motor-trucks. They work forty hours a week for £6/7/10, plus 9/- district allowance, plus 15/- camping put allowance. In those days we worked for a total of £5 a week, but in those days money went very much farther.

Blessed with mechanical transport, the staff of patrolmen and the flying gangs enjoy more "civilized" living conditions. Under Chief Inspector A. S. Wild, of the Agricultural Department, the most travelled man is Sub-Inspector Smith, who, in the old days, inspected the Number Two Fence from a buckboard drawn by two camels. Equipped now with a modern truck, he inspects every month the southern section of the Number One Fence, from the coast to Lake Nabberu, and more than half of the Number Two Fence, a total mileage of 1,032. Fence Number Three and the remainder of Number Two Fence are the responsibility of Sub-Inspector Lance Maddison, about whom I could write a book.

The country traversed by the great Number One Fence is most varied. Beginning at the Southern Ocean near Hopetoun, it rises from the sea up the face of a steep rock, and thence passes over the coast sand-dunes and across the vast and empty sand-plains on which the bush is barely a foot high. Here the country is gently undulating and there is no protection from the winds screaming hotly down from the north and hissing coldly from the south. Only the eagles know about the rabbits and the foxes lurking in the low bush which will tear a man's boots and leggings to shreds in less than a week's march.

The real scrub begins sixty or seventy miles from the sea, first in patches and belts, low and gradually becoming higher and more robust. There are no settlements in sight of the fence. Fire is the patrolman's greatest worry, for it will sweep fast under a strong west wind and creep slowly when the wind is gentle, like a cat stalking a mouse, and ready to spring at the call of the wind. The patrolman on this section had need to use horses in a larger dray loaded with chaff, for the ground feed is utterly useless for stock, and even camels would starve to death.

At about 100 miles from the coast the fence enters the southern extremity of the wheat lands, passing close to several huge granite rocks, acres in extent and rising several hundred feet. At the foot of these great rocks—smaller editions of Ayres Rock—the land is richer and supports acacias, creating a parkland aspect and a glory of daffodil yellow in springtime. The rain forms crystal pools on the summit of these rocks, and one wonders how it is that after the long hot summer, when not a drop of moisture remains on the rock, a few days after the water pools are formed they teem with tadpoles.

Farther north gums and wattles and wait-a-bit begin to appear among the low scrub, and these belts of real trees indicate good ground for cultivating wheat.

All the way to Burracoppin the numbers on the mile pegs have been coming down, to reach zero at the railway crossing the fence one mile east of this busy wheat town. Either side of the railway a road passes through the fence, and to-day the gateway spanning the main road is fitted with a magnificent ramp costing £250 to put down and doing away with the gate. Where the railway crosses there is an efficient pass-over with long wings of netting.

With exceptionally few angles the fence proceeds towards the far-distant northern coast. From the railway it passes up a long slope to enter a section of broken country before reaching the southern wheatlands of Lake Campion

At Lake Campion there is another rail crossing, and in my time the gates on either side of the railway were invariably left open. Both the camels and I were always happy to get away from these open wheatlands and the wheat traffic and enter the real salmon-gum forest of Lake Campion.

When first I passed through this magnificent forest of great gums with salmon-tinted trunks, and the smaller wattles flaming yellow in the spring, it presented to us a paradise. No matter how high the wind, how bitter cold in winter and shrivelling hot in summer, this forest provided shelter and shade. I was dismayed some two years afterwards on hearing the devil's noise of the axe, and, during the months which followed, spaces grew in the forest, and the trees crashed down, and the heat and the cold entered and destroyed that which we loved. And to-day, after all that destruction, the farms have been abandoned for lack of the rain which the trees brought, and no one can ever stand the salmon gums up again.

Sixty-five miles north of Burracoppin the fence departs from the forest to enter a desert of sand-plain having belts of jam-scrub laid upon low and completely useless desert bush, with here and there tortured swamp gums marking the course of a shallow creek. I name this a desert, despite correction from geographers, because no living thing exists excepting iguanas and flies and the bell bird which will trick you to thinking that a belled bullock is leading the team to camp. Even the crows won't stay inside this eighty-mile desert, for they would certainly starve to death. At each crossing a small party of crows would accompany us, camping at night nearby, cleaning up the dinner and breakfast refuse, and then hurrying along to catch up with us and remain with us all day as though fearful of being left behind.

The sand-plains give way to more robust scrub of mulga and pine. In summer the wind dies down for weeks together, and it is so silent by day and by night that often the patrolman will ring a camel bell or beat a tin just to relieve what appears to be pressure on his eardrums. From the pine and mulga country the fence enters the real grazing lands at about the 155-mile peg, and begins to pass over breakaway country which would delight the eye of any moving- picture cameraman.

Then to Dromedary Hill and the small homestead which once was the northern terminus of my section. This hill of three hundred-odd feet stands in the centre of a circular plain, and if the winter rains have fallen at the right time the entire surface of the little mountain is massed with buttercups, forming a great golden nugget upon the grey-green floor of the plain. And all about the plain, flowing to the lips of the breakaway, carpeting the square miles beneath the mulgas, are the everlasting daisies growing in huge patches of white and of yellow and of mauve. The hot summer winds come to tear the daisies away and lay bare the diamonds littering the earth—specks of mica.

After the lifeless desert comes the open country bearing saltbush and bluebush, broad and thin leafed mulgas, cotton bush and other feed. Sheep meander over paddocks square miles in area, and the rabbits and the kangaroos and the sulking foxes, the emus and the eagles and crows, all unite in giving a welcome.

In my day Dromedary Hill Station was owned by the Vermin Fence Department, and here were bred the camels to be used by the patrolmen. Then trucks came into use, and the camels were destroyed and the station was passed over to Narndee Sheep Station which adjoins it. The grass now has grown over the track encircling Dromedary Hill. We used to harness a couple of young camels to a heavy old dray and drive them round and round over that racecourse track, and when they were broken to the dray and amenable to reasoning, we would harness them first to a heavy buckboard and finally to a vehicle so light that one man could almost run with it. Round and round that nugget of gold we taught camels how to behave: when to stop and remain so, when to walk, when to jogtrot, and how to lie down and be harnessed or unharnessed without argument about it.

North of Dromedary Hill the fence continues to pass through fine pastoral country to Anketell Station, 240 miles from Burracoppin, and so to Jigalong Station, one-time headquarters for the northern section and now to be given over to the Inland Missions. And so to Lake Nabberu, which may be a lake once in every seven years, and where the fence surrounds gigantic sandhills and crosses great salt-bush plains which shimmer beneath the sun as though the entire earth were about to fly apart. Then on past the black Carnarvon Range. Spinifex covers the ground swells, and the wind find the rain have carved the hard cores of sandhills into fantastic shapes. There are no sheep and cattle here beside this section of fence, but there are the rabbits and the wild dogs, and this is a land beloved by the emus, the male birds sitting tight and raising seven, eight and ten chickens every year.

Lake Nabberu is 425 miles from Burracoppin, and almost 100 miles north of the Meekatharra-Wiluna railway crossing and road. But recently the fence north from Lake Nabberu to the coast, just south of the Eighty-mile Beach, has been abandoned by the Department, a length of 500 miles.

Shortage of men and of material dictated the decision to withdraw from this outer defence bastion and concentrate available forces on the remainder of the defensive system in depth. As a defence against the wave of rabbits it was never considered important, the rabbit apparently preferring the more temperate climate of the southern half of the continent for performing his migration feats. Only after consultation with the north-western Vermin Boards was the abandonment of this section decided upon.

For a State comprising almost a million square miles and so thinly populated, Western Australia has, indeed, done well to curb the inroads of migratory animals and the emu. The total mileage of its netted fence system of defence in depth against ground pests is 2,049. The annual cost to the taxpayer, including the recently abandoned north section of the Number One Fence, is £10,000, of which about £1,000 is contributed by farmers and pastoralists whose fences join the Fence. The Vermin Boards, which operate in districts, are in favour of this defensive system, and have been urging the erection of still another netted fence linking Number Two with Number One far south of the present confluence at Gum Creek.

TODAY the biggest enemy is not the rabbit but the emu. It comes in from the north-east as well as the east, arriving annually from the open spinifex plains and the sand-dunes country. Meeting with the netted barrier, flocks of hundreds come down southward.

What they can do to wheat crops is truly astonishing, trampling to destruction very much more than they eat. On one occasion their depredations to the farms about Lake Campion were so serious that the farmers asked for some military units with machine guns to deal with this pest. The resultant slaughter was heavy but not wholly successful because the birds would not wait to be mown down by machine-gun bullets but ran helter-skelter in all directions through the growing crops. It was also discovered that machine-gun bullets travel a long way, and were a positive menace to farmers and their workers and their stock.

Individual shooters are more successful. For every emu's head the Government will pay 3/-, whilst in addition the local Vermin Board will pay as much as 2/- and the farmers' organizations will add a further shilling. I wish those rates had ruled in my day on the Number One Vermin Fence.

13.

AUSTRALIAN GEOGRAPHICAL SOCIETY

TOWARD the end of August 1948, two much-travelled trucks and a bronzed party of six, led by Arthur W. Upfield, reached Perth after completing a 5,000-mile tour of the far north-west. The party included Michael Sharland, naturalist and journalist; J. K. Ewers, journalist; Ray Bean, *Walkabout's* staff photographer; Harry Tate, motor mechanic; and George King, cook.

The purpose of the tour was to obtain a comprehensive photographic record of the territory traversed and in particular the Kimberleys, and to gather information at first hand to enable a series of articles to be written covering physical features, industry, settlement, fauna, flora, etc.

The party, which had been two and a half months on the trip, had returned with what is regarded as the most outstanding collection of photographs yet taken in this distant territory, together with a great deal of information which will form the basis of many articles for publication in the Geographical Society's journal, *Walkabout*. The first of these articles will appear in either the November or December issue.

Heavy rains toward the end of June blocked the coastal road north of Carnarvon and made it necessary for the tour to begin at Kalgoorlie. The route northward was via Wiluna, Meekatharra (although not shown on map), Marble Bar and Port Hedland, and around the Eighty Mile Beach to Broome, where the party spent a day on a lugger, complete with pearl-divers. At Derby J. K. Ewers left the party for Yampi Sound (Cockatoo Island iron ore deposits), and a week later flew on to Wyndham and rejoined the tour.

From Derby the route led inland to Hall's Creek, thence via Turkey Creek to Wyndham. Unfortunately, the invitation of Rev. K. J. Coaldrake to visit Forrest River Mission (35 miles from Wyndham by launch) had to be cancelled on account of delays *en route*.

From Wyndham the party travelled south via Argyle Downs, Mistake Creek and Inverway Stations.

It was originally intended to negotiate the Canning Stock Route on the return journey, but advice received from both governmental and private sources indicated that trucks could not get through; consequently the return journey was made from Hall's Creek to Port Hedland and down the coastal route to Perth.

Walkabout Pays a Visit
Leone Biltris

When we first heard that the Australian Geographical Society was coming up to our part of the world I said wistfully, "Wouldn't it be great if they came through here?" George the stockman suggested, "Why not write and ask them to give us a look in?" "I couldn't do that," I said. "They will have their route planned and will probably be working to a schedule."

The Boss laughed. "This country doesn't take kindly to schedules," he said truthfully. "I'll bet before they're in the country a week they'll be a day or two behind. Go on; send a letter. They can only say No."

Rather doubtfully I wrote and said we would be very happy to see the party *if* by chance they were coming our way. And there the matter rested for a week or two.

The first excitement came when I received an answer thanking me and stating that Arthur W. Upfield and his party would he coming through on our route. We discussed the things of interest the party might like to hear, and we planned what we could give them to eat. But work had to go on, and out went the stock-camp for two weeks. Their parting injunction was: "If the *Walkabout* blokes come through, hang on to them till we get back, even if you have to steal their tyres."

That afternoon came a telegram over the telephone that connects us to our head station, the Ord River. The party was in Wyndham, and hoped to be here at the week-end. Just as I took the message, the Spring Creek plant, with Air Len Kiehne in charge, arrived for lunch. Hastily I told the book-keeper at the Ord, Mr Gosnel: "I'll ring you back later to send an answer."

I gave the men their dinner and sat on the stockyard rail while they saddled and rode the mettlesome colts that had just been broken and were on their first trip to the stock-camp. Then, when the small cavalcade had started off to join our plant, I betook me to the phone. It was dead.

ALL that day and all the following day I fiddled with wires and shook batteries and rang, but no answer came. At seven o'clock the following night I got through to the Ord. Air Gosnel sent the answering telegram over the pedal wireless at six- thirty the next morning. But after the eleven o'clock session he rang me to say the party had left Wyndham and the telegram was undelivered. That was a blow.

By the morning I was a little more cheerful. I told all the lubras, "You bin see 'em plenty dust longa Wyndham road, you bin sing out longa me." I inspected the small house and assured myself it was as tidy as it could possibly be short of moving everything out of it. And I settled down to wait.

Two days later there was a shout, "Truck bin come up longa Wyndham road, Alissus." One hasty dash to see that the kettle was boiling, another to make sure my hair was tidy, then out to the front gate. It was a drover going back to Hall's Creek. We gave him a meal and waved him on his way. Two hours later, another call. This must be they. We couldn't have two trucks in a day. This time it was a loading truck bound for the Ord.

We average maybe a truck a week here during the dry, though sometimes two or three weeks may pass without our seeing any. In five days that week I had seven trucks, and none of them the ones I was waiting for.

ON Monday a boy rode in from the stock-camp to say they would be in a few days early. They had a mob of cattle and were bringing them in to the station to draft and brand up. I could expect them on Wednesday.

That afternoon I told the girls they could go walkabout for a few hours. Cocky, my kitchen girl, demanded, "What name this mans bin come up longa two trucks? Where him be—ey? Alla time we bin look about, him no more bin come. What's the matter longa we, he don't bin come?"

"Never mind," I comforted her. "Alight be they bin come up this afternoon." Cocky's lip jutted out. "Well, might be I no more bin look alonga him," she said in disgust. "I bin go alonga river bin have 'im bogey."

The girls departed and I tried to concentrate on some knitting. Suddenly I heard a sound and walked on to the verandah. Two neat blue trucks were coming through the gate. I forgot the kettle, my hair could have been like a birch broom and I wouldn't have known or cared. All I could say to myself was, "They're here, and it's Monday evening. Perhaps they'll wait until the boys come."

I went to the gate to meet them. And there entered through the gate six men who in just a few short hours became part of our family: Messrs Upfield, Sharland, Ewers, Tate, Bean, and King. It took me until lunchtime the following day to get their names sorted out, but it took me only about ten minutes to pass inward judgment. "Nice fellows."

I asked them how long they could stay, and they said they were nearly a week late as it was. I thought of the Boss' words, said hopefully, "But a week's nothing up here," and threw in the only bribe I had to offer. "The boys will be in with a decent mob of cattle on Wednesday. You may get some good photographs." After a cup of tea Mr Upfield held a brief consultation with the rest of his party and they decided they would stay the night and try to get out to the stock-camp by truck the following day.

I might say here that Mistake Creek is rather primitive. Until last year there had never been a white woman on it; consequently most of the small amenities so necessary to a home were lacking. We have little in the way of comfort to offer the stranger who stays with us. But it didn't worry our party one scrap. They were a perfectly self-contained unit. Three of the men brought in their beds and set them up on our wide, flagstoned verandah. The other three elected to sleep out under the stars and set up their beds right at our front gate. I wonder if they knew they were really sleeping on the main Wyndham road?

I introduced them all to the rakish bough shed that constitutes our bathroom. I initiated them into the intricate mysteries of our primitive shower that falls with the least provocation on top of the head of unwary persons using it. I completely forgot the plans we had made for the entertaining of the party; forgot too the intelligent, interesting information that was to be tendered carelessly.

How could I remember these things when the party was six happy-go-lucky men, just like our own men on the station, and interested in everything? They trooped down to the kitchen that night to watch me set the bread. They were there in the morning to see it being "knocked back," and again when I was tinning it up. They were there, cameras in hand, when my girls were putting it in the old brick oven. We discussed everything under the sun: books and people, politics and plays, the country, the natives, and the refrigerator that is on its way to this station and eagerly awaited.

JUST before lunch one truck prepared to go out to the stock-camp with my old donkey driver as guide. They had not reached the gate when we who had remained saw the three horsemen coming down the track. I hoped desperately for a miracle. The truck reached the horsemen and stopped. Two men swung off their horses and climbed on to the running board of the truck. The truck turned for home and I sighed with relief. The impossible had happened. The miracle had been duly delivered. The camp, with a big mob in hand, was home. Mr Upfield's generous wait had not been in vain.

The old house erupted into vigorous life. Eleven men sat down with me to supper that night. We had a new table. It only arrived a couple of months ago, with six chairs. The first chairs on the place. As the table was too big for our small gauzed dining-room, we had put it in the front room, and I had often lamented that we never had enough people present to use it. Our dining-room table seats ten. But on this night of nights we christened the new table. It took the combined efforts of my two biggest tablecloths to cover it, and we didn't have nearly enough serviettes to go round. But that didn't matter a scrap. There was laughter and good fellowship at the table, and food for all. Who could possibly want more than that?

It was a memorable and an hilarious evening. Our party told us some of their experiences in other far-away places. The boys swapped yarns about cattle and cattlemen. I thanked heaven that the roof was nailed securely; otherwise the laughter that rose must surely have lifted it clean off the rafters. We listened to the muted beats of the didgeridoo that came drifting from the camp, and over and above the night came the bawling of the cattle in the yards and the restless stamping of their feet.

That night there were beds scattered all around our three verandahs and outside our gate. Voices called through the crisp darkness and other voices answered. My two little puppies, only two months old and quite unused to many people about, nearly wore their small pads out, hurrying from one fondling hand to another; and, I regret to state, scurrying off with an odd sock or two.

But silver moons give way to golden days. By daylight our boys had had a hurried breakfast and were in the yards drafting. The breakfast party was reinforced by two men who arrived on a loading truck from Darwin. That made the company fourteen in all. A nice, satisfactory number to see about a table.

Regretfully I watched the party packing up after breakfast; wishing they could stay another month, a week, or even a day. But time was precious and they couldn't even stay for lunch. There was a last muster of all hands at eight-thirty when I took the smoke-o up to the men at the stockyards, Mr Upheld gallantly carrying the bucket of tea and a bucket of pannikins while I carried the cakes and biscuits. Everybody sat or stood around in a cloud of dust from the yards and drank tea out of pint-sized enamel mugs. The boys were extending pleading and sincere invitations to the party to stay for the Negri race meeting, which takes place the first week in September.

It was useless, however, and goodbyes had to be said. Hearty handclasps were all that were left, and we couldn't say half the things that were in our hearts. There was a last wave, and a cloud of dust; then the gate was closed and our guests were gone. Did I say guests? No, these men were not our guests. They were our very good friends. And because they were our friends we did not have to worry about making them comfortable. They took us just as we were. I think they knew how happy we were to have them, and I hope they know just how much pleasure we had in their company. They were only with us a short two days in time, but they are really a part of this country and this life now. They slipped into our lives as though they had always belonged there. They were part of our family and took their share of the jokes and the sly witticisms with hearty good humour. We speak of them now intimately, as we speak of old and tried friends. The boys summed it up in fewer words, and far more eloquently than I ever could when they said appreciatively, "Well, what a mob of nice blokes."

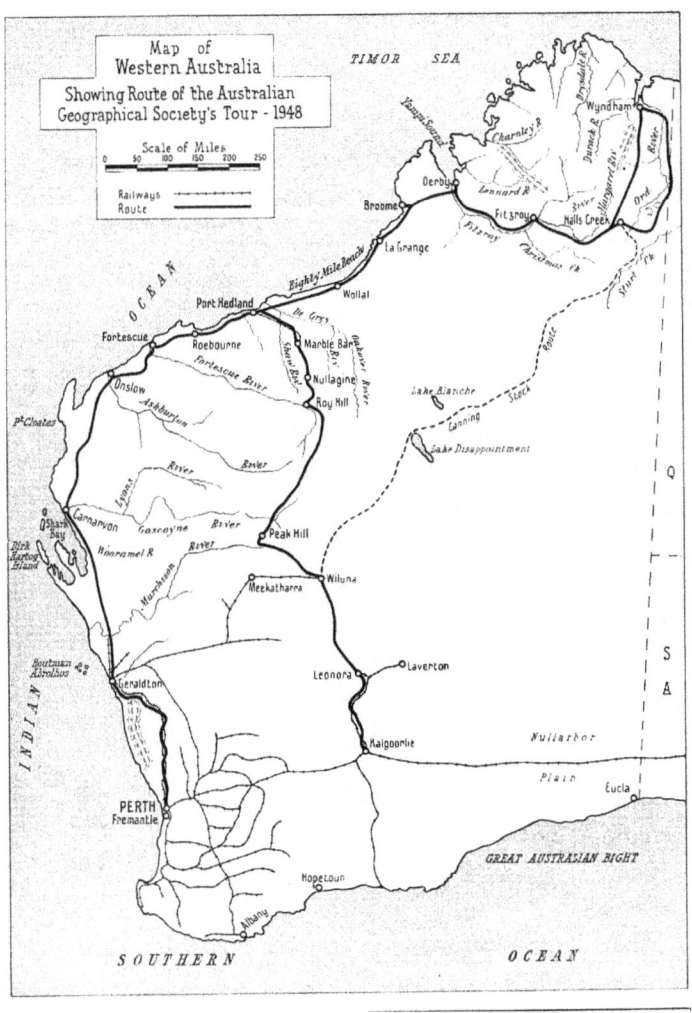

ACKNOWLEDGEMENTS

The publisher would like to thank William and Francesca Upfield for suggesting this idea for a book. The original publication dates in *Walkabout* for these stories are as follows:

Arthur Upfield: An Epitaph by Pamela Ruskin, May 1 1964.
1 Patrolling the World's Longest Fence, March 1 1935.
2 A Visit to Lake Frome, December 1 1934.
3 Men, Sheep and Far Horizons, January 1 1935.
4 Hosts hidden in the Bush, February 1 1935
5 Coming Down With Cattle, November 1 1934.
6 An Australian Camel Station, June 1 1935.
7 Trapping for Fur, September1 1935.
8 Angling for Swordfish, February 1 1942.
9 This Jealous Land, April 1 1948.
10 Walking the Cattle, May 1 1948.
11 Pearling Town of the North-West, March 1 1949.
12 The Vermin Fences of Western Australia, May 1 1949.
13 Australian Geographical Society, October 1 1948.

Other Titles by Arthur W. Upfield and published by ETT Imprint:

1 The House of Cain
2 The Beach of Atonement
3 A Royal Abduction
4 Gripped by Drought
5 Breakaway House
6 The Murchison Murders
7 The Gifts of Frank Cobbold
8 The Great Melbourne Cup Mystery
9 Follow My Dust
10 Up & Down Australia
11 Up & Down the Real Australia
12 Up & Down Australia Again
13 Beyond the Mirage;
14 Walkabout

forthcoming
Bony at Bermagui

Upfield's own drawing of Bony

Bony Novels by Upfield:

1 The Barrakee Mystery
2 The Sands of Windee
3 Wings Above the Diamantina
4 Mr Jelly's Business
5 Winds of Evil
6 The Bone is Pointed
7 The Mystery of Swordfish Reef
8 Bushrangers of the Skies
9 Death of a Swagman
10 The Devil's Steps
11 An Author Bites the Dust
12 The Mountains Have a Secret
13 The Widows of Broome
14 The Bachelors of Broken Hill
15 The New Shoe
16 Venom House
17 Murder Must Wait
18 Death of a Lake
19 The Cake in the Hat Box
20 The Battling Prophet
21 Man of Two Tribes
22 Bony Buys a Woman
23 Bony and the Mouse
24 Bony and the Black Virgin
25 Bony and the Kelly Gang
26 Bony and the White Savage
27 The Will of the Tribe
28 Madman's Bend
29 The Lake Frome Monster

www.ingramcontent.com/pod-product-compliance
Lightning Source LLC
Chambersburg PA
CBHW032126090426
42743CB00007B/489